HOW TO RETURN JUST ABOUT ANYTHING

HOW TO RETURN JUST ABOUT ANYTHING

Patricia Forst

THOMAS NELSON PUBLISHERS
Nashville

Published in Nashville, Tennessee, by Oliver-Nelson Books, a division of Thomas Nelson, Inc., Publishers, and distributed in Canada by Lawson Falle, Ltd., Cambridge, Ontario.

Library of Congress Cataloging-in-Publication Data

Forst, Patricia, 1946–
How to return just about anything / Patricia Forst.
p. cm.
ISBN 0-8407-9645-5 (paperback)
1. Returning goods. 2. Customer service.
3. Consumer satisfaction. I. Title.
HF5415.5.F67 1992
640—dc20 92-34245
CIP

Printed in the United States of America
1 2 3 4 5 — 95 94 93 92

Contents

Introduction

THE WHITE ELEPHANT THEORY

THE BIGGEST DETERRENT TO TAKING BACK AN ITEM THAT IS NOT SUITABLE TO OUR NEEDS IS THAT WE HAVE LOST OUR RECEIPT!

Many of us have countless items that will occupy space in our homes forever because the items did not meet our needs and we did not know that we have a store-given right to return them. That happens all the time because we tend to think that our buying moments are finished with the sale. Very often when we make an innocent buying mistake, we think that we have a moral obligation to keep the items.

Reputable storekeepers care about their customers. They want their customers to feel at home in their stores. They want their customers to feel that the sales are not over until they are satisfied with the services that the stores have provided. When you become more aware of your rights as a responsible consumer, you will realize that a store is truly concerned with your satisfaction and that every reputable store provides the consumer with the right to return!

The store does it as a service to the consumer but also as a method to ensure your repeat business. Reputable stores fear not the loss of a sale but the loss of a customer. A simple return represents the loss of a few dollars, but an unhappy customer means the loss of repeat business over a period of years. A business can*not* survive on occasional and sporadic sales. The merchants who represent reputable establishments want to nurture community relationships one customer at a time.

They are building a reputation one customer at a time. It is the merchants' business to know that the shopping process is difficult and that although they (the storekeepers) are experts in their field, the customers can*not* be expected to be consumer experts. The storekeepers have spent years learning their businesses and marketing techniques. They know that the consumers are busy earning their livelihoods in their own areas of expertise. They want the shopping public to know without a shadow of a doubt that the merchants are aware of the consumers' needs. They try hard to provide a shopping environment that will please and satisfy their customers again and again. The storekeepers design their return-it policies for "satisfaction guaranteed"! And if we frequent stores that have designed these policies for our convenience, we will be rewarded with the shopping experience that they wish to provide for us, the customers.

Your Right to Return

It is your store-given right to return, and the stores second it. In fact, they "first" it because the stores designed the policies for your convenience!

Recently, we were visiting my dad, a spry eighty-two-year-old who, following the loss of my mom, has been undaunted in his efforts to be self-sufficient and independent. He was very happy to see us and relayed his day's activities from his housecleaning chores to his laundry accomplishments, and then with a puzzled look and a shake of his head he said, "I've done really well with my newfound grocery shopping activities and microwave lessons. But I bought a Sunday shirt (a long-sleeved white shirt for church), and it just doesn't fit! The neck is too big, and my tie looks funny!

"Can you use it, Jack? It's yours if you can use it. I hate to see a perfectly good shirt go to waste. I would love you to have it!"

Without a moment of hesitation, Jack and I said, "Return it, Dad!"

Dad said, "Oh, no, it's okay. . . . You take it if it fits you. Or give it to Scott (our fourteen-year-old son)."

After thanking him and telling him that it was very sweet of him to offer, we said, "But, Dad, you should return it. The store will exchange it for you! Or you can get your money back if it does not have your size."

"Oh . . . I don't know," said Dad. "I've taken it completely apart. I have the plastic bag, but the cardboard is out of the collar. We'll see," he said.

The next evening Dad called to say, "Well, you were right. They took my shirt back. I put the shirt on a hanger, and I put all the tissue paper and the shirt bag and the cardboard and the pins into the store bag and took it all back with my receipt. They had another shirt. And the saleswoman was so nice to me. That's really great!" he said. "I really didn't know I could do that. It's a big help. I'll shop there all the time."

This was a pure case of "satisfaction guaranteed" by a reputable store for a deserving customer, who appreciated his right to return so much that he plans to be a regular customer at that store.

Purchases Aren't Irreversible

Dad had the store-given right to return at a reputable store, whether he knew it or not! Whether Dad used his right to return or not, a reputable store provides the right and welcomes a legitimate return. Many people, particularly senior citizens, tend to feel that a purchase that does not meet their intended need—even when they have their receipt—is an irreversible purchase.

Very often that concept is a carryover from the days when many of their purchases were not packaged but personalized and procured in a neighborhood environment where they felt at home naturally. It was easy in the neighborhood environment to feel comfortable enough to tell the butcher that "Sunday's roast was a little tough," and know without having to say a word that he would throw in an extra lamb chop this week to compensate for the grainy roast last week. By the same token, they shopped at general stores where they bought yard goods that were cut just for them and sewn at home by Mom or Grandmom.

> ***A reputable store welcomes a legitimate return.***

Those were days when "satisfaction guaranteed" was achieved not necessarily by a return but through a "this for that" type of compensation, a balance of now and later. Generally speaking, those types of buying situations do not apply to today's shopping environment because the neighborhood store concept has given way to the large multifaceted shopping mall. We are a mobile, fast-moving society of people who can extend neighborhoods fifty miles by traveling to the biggest mall if we have the horsepowered engine to get us there!

Nevertheless, just as the local butcher would have personally assured the quality of his meat and the sanctity of his word, so, too, do reliable stores guarantee the quality of their products and the reliability of their establishments.

By very definition, malls can be overwhelming for a shopper, but they have blossomed in our society because just as a farmer is dictated to by the seasons, so, too, merchants and shoppers are controlled by the dictates of today's times. We are an "around-the-clock type of society" whose needs must be served quickly (when leisure is not an option) or leisurely (when relaxation is the customer's purpose), and all in an atmosphere that makes shopping an efficient and satisfactory experience for you as a customer and the merchants as businesspeople. The key here is a partnership created by the merchants and the consumer to work together for a common goal, that is, the merchants' livelihoods and your efficient, timely, and ultimately successful shopping experience.

"Ultimately successful" is an important description

in the shopping process because success and satisfaction are not always immediate. In today's shopping environment the store owners, managers, and salespeople can*not* possibly know you as personally as the general store managers knew their customers. They can*not* serve you in quite the same fashion that the store owners used to be able to serve your grandparents. The store owners were everything to everyone.

However, in view of this fact, today's merchants recognize the even greater need to make you feel "at home" in your neighborhoods while you are shopping at modern-day malls. Let them protect you! Let them provide that good old-fashioned service with "satisfaction guaranteed"!

Don't be afraid to return something when you have a problem. Take pride in the fact that reputable storekeepers know that open shopping policies provide a needed customer service that breeds trust and great customer relations for the long run. That is why most stores call the business office the CUSTOMER SERVICE DEPARTMENT.

Your Happy Shopping Experience

A big plus for today's shopping environment is that your happy shopping experience can easily and efficiently extend as far as Maine or Florida through catalog shopping or as near as your corner drugstore or food market.

A friend of mine relayed the story of a little grandmotherly woman who walked up to the customer service counter of our local food chain, with cheeks as red (from embarrassment) as the watermelon that she was holding, and said, "You'll think I'm crazy for returning a watermelon. I know it cost only $3.99, but it tastes awful. And my little granddaughter has been looking forward to coming to my house for a picnic and watermelon!"

As she sputtered and apologized, the store manager escorted her over to the vegetable and fruit department. He began to cut open watermelons. He smiled and said, "We'll find one that tastes like summer!"

He went on to say that he really appreciated the fact that she had come all the way back to the store to let him know about the melon because store communications with the customers meant a lot to him. He also mentioned that he thought her little granddaughter had a pretty special Grandma! You might say, "His reputation was on the vine!"

Dad and the little woman had such respect for the system that they almost gave up their store-given right to return items that did not meet their needs. They were not totally aware of their rights, and therefore, they could have made a buying mistake that could have cost them hard-earned dollars. Most people can*not* afford to lose these dollars, and they need to take advantage of the store's self-appointed return policies, but it is refreshing to note that the two senior citizens were very concerned not to take one shirt pin or piece of melon that they were not entitled to have!

That approach is necessary when people have a respect for one another, a real and legitimate problem, and a legitimate desire to resolve the problem fairly in the interests of both the store and the consumer. Generally speaking, both parties are interested in fair and equitable solutions to shopping problems that may occur.

In returning an item, the consumer has a responsibility to exercise shopping rights in a fair and just matter. That is honorable and protects the rights. The store has an obligation to be fair to the consumer and to provide and honor the rights.

The Consumer's Side

Only shop at stores that honor the consumer with fair return policies, but always keep in mind that for the system to work, half of the process falls clearly on the consumer's shoulders. Honesty, integrity, fairness, courtesy—the consumer should abide by these basics in dealing with salespersons and in returning merchandise.

> ***The consumer has a responsibility to exercise shopping rights in a fair and just manner.***

The consumer's half of the bargain usually requires that merchandise be returned in "like-new" condition (unless of course it is a quality problem on an item that has already been used but is guaranteed for a certain length of time). Merchandise should be returned in its original packaging. Merchandise should be returned in a timely manner. (Look for the store's posted policy.)

Merchandise should be returned with a receipt. These requirements are not irreversible, but they are what the stores generally require and what they are entitled to expect you to have for a money-back return.

Often the store will willingly make exceptions to the rules, but it is the store's choice. You are placing yourself at the store's mercy (which in many cases is not strained); it's definitely no longer your store-given right if you are missing one of the posted elements of the store's return policy!

The one prerequisite that seems to be a constant and reasonable requirement for these returns is a receipt. It is a necessary element of proof for the store's records to keep the accounts and inventory balanced, and it is the one element that most people usually toss aside. Consequently, the nameless unwanted items are in our homes and garages forever through no merit of their own but merely because we did not understand our right to return.

If the merchants realize the need, in the future so should you! A buying mistake is correctable, and the process is acceptable and endorsed by the store if you have your receipt!

Unsuitable Items

The items are not "near and dear" to our hearts. Nevertheless, they are ours forever if we do not take them back in a timely fashion with the receipt. How does this happen?

Has this ever happened to you? Have you ever rented space to a White Elephant? Of course you have! We all have given shelter to White Elephants.

White Elephant—any article, big or small, that seems to take up pachydermal space and stomp around in all the wrong places of your home because when you realized that it wasn't suitable to your needs, you didn't have a receipt to RETURN IT!

"It" now has White Elephant status forever in your home because you weren't prepared to return it—much like an uninvited guest who happens to be your long-lost crotchety, but rich, uncle.

You would like to get rid of it. Come to think of it, you would like to get rid of him, too! "Begone annoying guest! Leave us!" But alas! Who could justify the loss?

One might say that being without a receipt for a White Elephant is like having a dying uncle who has enjoyed poor health for forty years and outlives you and the White Elephant!

The moral of this story is that with the price of groceries these days, we can*not* afford to feed, house, and pay rent for White Elephants! When we are not prepared to make a timely return, we are left with an uninvited guest who has moved in forever, and then we must go out and spend more money to buy what we really wanted in the first place.

That doesn't have to happen to you if you learn your shopper's rights and exercise them responsibly!

CHAPTER 1

WHY DIDN'T YOU BUY WHAT YOU WANTED?

WHY DIDN'T YOU BUY WHAT YOU WANTED TO BUY IN THE FIRST PLACE?

Most of the items that we take back do not necessarily go back because we don't like them, don't want them, couldn't use them, or just hate them.

In fact I often regret having to take back some of my favorite items because through no fault of mine, they break, don't match (bookends), won't cook (popcorn), bite (mean dog).

When Things Break—Be Reassured

An item might decide not to heat up (coffeepot), not to run (new car), to stick (zipper), to catch on fire (television), to lose its mind (computer), not to keep time, and generally speaking, drive you out of your mind!

During the day, you can be sure that your list of things to do will be taller than you.

In the course of getting up, getting out the door, parenting, sitting in traffic, earning a living, life's not forgiving.

But when things break, it's comforting to know that out the door you can go to take them back.

Time Stealers

The unexpected is always there to steal your time and boggle your mind! The car's been towed! Chicken pox . . . "Oh, no!" Service people who never show! Broken washers! Machines that "grind"! All of these can put you behind.

Then there are all those exterior forces that put you back to the Age of Horses—ice, snow, sleet, hail, floods, earthquakes, and subway strikes. "Yikes!" (They're after you.)

Those "hidden forces" in every day that make our choices go astray—layoffs, broken nails, unemployment, too? Who would ever know the demands placed upon you in the course of a normal day?

Demands on Our Time

There are thousands of demands placed upon our time by society, the family, and ourselves.

We allow precious time for reading a book, learning to cook, making family dinners, seeing movies, parental bonding, and taking vacations.

The everyday commonplace joys can be severely limited by meetings, business greetings, practices for sports, yard work, maintenance, doctors, dentists, too!

There is so much to do that shopping just isn't a pleasurable thing for you.

A Shopper's Pace

During your shopping time, which is severely limited by external forces, there is no guarantee that in your space of time—that small "window" in mall space time (like the windows of outer space)—you will be able to zero in on exactly what you are looking for!

You may not be the Lottery Winner in the Shirt Search or the Jacket Picker Person of the Week!

Perhaps you'll fall short of the Shining Sheet Searcher Award or the Royal Winner of the Quest for the Perfect Tool Chest!

Especially since you must do it all in between picking up Susie from ballet, fixing the roof, getting new tires, taking Uncle Ed to the doctor, walking the dog, couponing, exercising, teacher conferencing, grocery shopping, mopping, all without stopping.

These events in life are the answer to the question, "Why didn't you buy what you thought you would when you were there and thought you could?"

CHAPTER 2

THE RIGHT AND THE RECEIPT

The process of returning involves two main areas.

We can refer to them as the two *R*'s—the *right* and the *receipt!* They are like love and marriage, tea for two, in and out, left and right. You can't have one without the other.

The *receipt* involves the how to do it. It's the foundation for the mechanics of returning.

The other half of the team is the *right* to take it back. The right is the realization that in the entire shopping process we are in control of our purse strings before, during, and after the sale.

We are all aware of our right to buy after the selection process has been completed, but we must become aware of our right to return after the buying process.

Your receipt is the foundation for the mechanics of returning.

The right is the knowledge that you can do it!!!! The guts to go back to the store. The understanding that returning is part of the buying process. Returning is supposed to happen. We must learn to think in terms of the sale or the shopping not being over until *we* are completely satisfied with the purchase. This satisfaction should involve the quality of the purchase, the reliability of the purchase, the performance of the purchase, the need for the purchase, the purpose of the purchase.

In simple dollars and cents (or is it dollars and sense?) that means, Does it work right all the time the way it should when you need it to do what you bought it to do?

Quality

The quality of the purchase often involves a predetermined time factor during which the item is guaranteed against defect and is expected to perform at a reasonable level of service.

The quality of an item will bring you back to repurchase the item when you are ready, and it will encourage you to purchase another type of product from that same company. Therefore, it goes without saying that manufacturers of reputable merchandise usually provide for the quality control of their products with warranties and guarantees. They protect you and the companies' reputations.

Once again it is up to the store and the consumer to be partners in explaining and honoring the terms of the quality agreements.

> ***Satisfaction should involve quality, reliability, performance, need, and purpose.***

Reliability

The reliability of the product is directly related to how often it does what it is supposed to do and how well it does it. It is all about dependability! Here, too, we have a time factor. Unless the purchase is of a disposable nature, there will be a reasonable amount of time during which you obviously need to save your receipt in order to go back to the store with a quality or reliability problem. Timely returns are of the essence for the consumer and the store when the customer has an immediate problem with the merchandise, but you can see that you still need to save your receipt for proof in case a problem arises later with the quality or reliability of that same product. You must have your proof of purchase to show the store that it was in fact the store's merchandise. The receipt indicates the date of purchase and the store from which the item was purchased. That allows the manufacturer to document records in response to your complaint. Even though your warranty and guarantee cards from the manufacturer are filled out and mailed in at the time of purchase, some companies request the items to be returned with your receipt since the warranties and guarantees are usually extended only to the original customer.

Most of the items that we are discussing in this category are larger ticket items that are usually identified on a receipt with an invoice number, a description, a model number, the store where the item was purchased, and the name, address, and telephone number of the customer. It is very simple to validate your original ownership by showing the company a copy of your original receipt. The company will compare it to their warranty or guarantee card and notify you how they will handle the problem.

For example, many of the better vacuum cleaner companies, for a very small fee, offer an opportunity to send your machine back to the factory to be refurbished every two years. The offer is usually explained in the small print on the warranty page of the owner's manual. A copy of the manual's warranty page and some form of identification to show that you are the original owner are all you need to qualify for this opportunity. There will never be a question concerning your eligibility if you have the original receipt and a copy of the warranty page of your manual. The manual will list the model number and the date of purchase and the receipt will say that the manual is yours.

The same procedure simplifies returns on defective items, too. I returned a very expensive pair of golf shoes to the manufacturer because the soles split at the seams. I sent a copy of the original receipt and our present address. Within a week, I had a letter telling me that they were very sorry about my problem and that they would be repairing and returning my shoes. Within two weeks they had completely resoled the shoes and returned them to me with a check for the postage that I had paid. You can usually get the names and addresses of the companies from your portion of the warranty or guarantee cards, but if you have lost or misplaced your portion of the card, you can get the information from the store where you purchased the item or any store that carries the brand.

Performance

Performance is an easier and more timely characteristic used to measure the worth of a product because you can usually see if the item accomplishes the task for which you purchased it within the usual thirty-day period that most stores allow for a timely return. If the performance diminishes after that time, it will usually be a quality or reliability problem.

Need and Purpose

The need and the purpose for which you buy the product are closely related but somewhat different in nature. The need for a product may be real and apparent, but that does not always mean it can be satisfied. You may have a sofa that needs a replacement pillow.

The sofa needs a pillow, but you may not be able to find the right shade of beige to match the other cushions. You may need to make returns several times before you can satisfy the need. That is a legitimate reason for return even though you still need the product after you have returned it. Eventually, you may find the perfect pillow for your sofa, but in a week the lining may slip and cause the pillow to sag.

Suddenly, the pillow matches the color of your sofa, but it doesn't fulfill the purpose for which you bought it. Now the pillow is uncomfortable, and it looks sloppy on your sofa. Obviously, you need to take it back, and you are entitled to return it because you have a legitimate complaint. Reliable stores will want to serve you and complete the purpose for which you purchased the product.

Now we can see that these decisions cannot always be made at the moment or in the moments immediately following the purchase. On the other hand, people too often assume that the purchase was made in heaven, and blessed by the salesperson. They are pleased with the idea of the purchase. They are certain that it is perfect. They love the color, and they feel that this could quite possibly be their finest hour of shopping. In the enjoyment and delight of their buying moment, they throw down the receipt as they leave the store. They leave the receipt at the cashier's desk to be thrown out in the evening's trash. They examine the receipt, smile, and then promptly toss the proof of purchase over their shoulders as an affirmation of the purchase! Very often people rip open their bags, pull out their purchases, and forget about their receipts! They OOOOooooh and

AHHHHhhhh over their buying moment, and in the meantime their receipts have flown onto the floor, out the car door, down the street, where they and their receipts shall never meet again!

A man snoring in his bed a mile away has a better chance of inhaling those elusive receipts—as they wing into his open bedroom window on a gust of wind—than they will ever have of finding those little pieces of documentation from the bottom of a ripped bag that contained the purchase of their dreams.

Of course you should be pleased with your buying side of the shopping adventure! Certainly kick up your heels on the escalator ride to the store door because you got the sale of the century, the deal of the year, the coup of the buying world, the only one left on the planet, the only size two in the Northern Hemisphere, the best one ever made, a "real" antique, a perfect match, the exact shade of purple, a sale on a sofa sectional for the left-hand side of the room (or was it the right?)!

HHHHMMMMmmmm! Left? . . . Right? . . . Wait a minute! LEFT? . . . RIGHT? . . . WAIT A MINUTE!

Suddenly, by the time you reach the car, the interstate, the bus, or the subway, you shout, "STOP THAT CASH REGISTER!"

You just discovered this century is coming to an end! It's last year's model! It's obsolete! It's the only one left because the plug is broken! The purple is perfect, but the zipper is broken! The shoes match the purse, but the heels are scuffed! The pillow is soft, but there's a pull in the seam! It's upsetting enough that you could scream!

But wait, life's great! 'Cause you did save the receipt.

You didn't throw away the bag. You resisted the urge to confirm your satisfaction with your purchase by crushing the original packaging.

Importance of Receipts

Hooray! What a day! We're beginning to see what a great buddy, friend, necessity, condition, asset, requirement, prerequisite a receipt can be!

You can refer to it as a permission slip because without it there is usually no trip to the Land of Returning.

Yes, of course you are right! It isn't impossible to return without a receipt, but it's tough!

You can expect to run into all the negative reactions you would get whenever you go anywhere without the things you are supposed to have to get where you want to be to do what you need to do.

> ***It isn't impossible to return without a receipt, but it's tough!***

I call it my Tough to List. It's tough to get a ticket to the Superbowl at the gate (not impossible . . . tough to). It's tough to get a loan without collateral. It's tough to have macaroni without cheese. It's tough to fish without a hook. It's tough to cook without heat. It's tough to fly without wings. It's tough to get milk without a cow. But the moral of the story is, if you save your receipts, that will never happen to you now!

The key to applying the method is proof. In the Land of Returning the key to the city is proof, proof, and more proof!

How do you gather this proof? Be the Sherlock Holmes of receipts. Save, file, and check your receipts. That is all the proof you will need!

Proof validates your right. We all have the right and the need to return, but like fric and frac, bread and butter, you can't have one without the other. Proof is the basis of the process.

Rule 1: You must never give up your right to return.

Rule 2: You can protect your right to return only by proof (receipts).

Rule 3: Return it responsibly.

If proof is the foundation, then the actual return is the finished product. If you don't know why you're saving receipts when the time comes to act and return, you won't return it. You'll wait till the cows come home, which could be never! Rumor has it that despite the fact that your average cows have the look of real intelligence shining in their big brown eyes, their tests from their "dairy preschools" indicate that they would have trouble and probably would never be able to find their own way home. (Why else would the farmers of America put up all those fences?) Historically, the cows of Europe have had the right of way while crossing roads because if they had to stop for cars, they would forget where they were going. The moral of the story is, you must know what you intend to do with your receipt when you have a need to return.

Once you understand the Charlotte Russe Theory of

Proof, you will understand the concept of Receipt =Right! You will then be ready to see its application to the method or the Keeping Track Theory.

I will give you some strategies that will provide you with methods to protect your right to return. These methods are the means.

This book is really about your thinking. If you think about your right to return, if you are convinced of your right to actually do it, if you know how to do it, *How to Return Just About Anything* will become your SHOPPING BIBLE!

CHAPTER 3

THE CHARLOTTE RUSSE THEORY

Wouldn't it be nice to be a confident shopper who knows how to buy wisely and return confidently?

I believe I can show you an efficient and fair method to become an educated return-it person!

As a teenager, I can remember going to the bank for my mother, and as I raced down the front steps, she called to me, "Don't talk to strangers! Do you have change for the bus? Bring the receipt from the bank!"

I remember thinking to myself, *I know. I have. Why?* But I had a healthy respect for my mother's requests so the *why* didn't really matter. There was also a real advantage to keeping my bank job because I was rewarded with a quarter for a charlotte russe.

Proof is called the Charlotte Russe Theory!

Charlotte russe—guaranteed to be without caloric content, this confectionary delight of swirly whipped cream mounded over a boring (but delicious) cake is held together by a little cardboard holder (that is why there are no calories). The holder enables it to fit perfectly into the hand of a sweet-toothed person, and it absorbs the calories and carbohydrates! In 1960, in Bayonne, New Jersey, it cost exactly 25¢. The caloric guarantee lasts until age forty when according to my mom and any good mom of any ethnic origin, "All that junk food catches up to you, and you gain twenty-five pounds!"

I could be motivated by a goody. As a matter of fact, I know that my return-it techniques will work for just about anyone because I have never been a financial wizard, and they work for me. I received an allowance of 25¢ a week for the first six years of my elementary school career. In all that time I never spent it on anything but candy. I spent 5¢ a day at Sam's Candy Store or the school candy counter. Therefore, it is obvious that my talents were bending not to the world of "high finance" but to the "sweeter, gentler" things of life.

An Amazing Discovery

We all grow up, however, and as I went into the world to earn a living, I made some amazing discoveries. One was the answer to the question, Why save your mom's bank receipt?

> ***Return-it techniques will work for just about anyone.***

Believe it or not, sometimes bank officials do lose track of who puts money into their institutions. Consequently, if you do not save your receipt, you can*not* prove that you deposited any money.

Fairly obvious? Actually not! I have observed people throw away their bank receipts just the way they throw down their sales receipts.

"Impossible," you say.

Believe me, that old adage "Momma knows best" is based in total fact and my experience the hard way!

Allow me to explain. After my first month of teaching, when I was old enough to be on my own and not forced to pay attention to little details like bank receipts, I opened an account at the local bank where my parents had been doing business for years. I felt comfortable there. It was the bank that kept me in charlotte russe money.

Little did I know that they knew me, but to them, my account was just a NUMBER! They didn't know me from ADAM'S HOUSE CAT.

Adam's house cat—the cat that lived in Adam's house (Adam and Eve's house, that is!). We all know the story of Adam and Eve, but no one has ever given us the particulars on their personal lives other than their taste in fruit and their inability to manage their children. Consequently, it wouldn't seem unlikely that their house cat became the unwitting victim of anonymity and a symbol of anything or anyone unknown. When was the last time that *People* magazine did a spread on or the local Bible study group held a discussion about the not-so-famous Adam's house cat?

Nevertheless, without cause or reason, I felt like the whole world knew me and respected me enough to know without question that I was totally trustworthy and, consequently, someone who obviously did not need to save receipts.

Besides, the bank would never make a mistake with my money! Would it?

Well, if it made a tiny mistake, the tellers would know immediately that I was telling the truth about my deposit. Wouldn't they?

We will see!

"You Have No Money!"

One Friday after school I realized that if I was really going to have a great weekend (which is everyone's parting wish for the employees of America), I had better drive my hot new Mustang out of the parking lot and into the drive-in line at the bank. I was going to New York—The City! I would need cash (even then a trip to New York was somewhat like a holdup).

I pulled up to the window and wrote my check with

a pen I borrowed from the teller. OOPS! Needless to say, the teller was already irritated with me. But suddenly, he stopped, looked over his glasses and, with an even more authoritarian twitch of his lips, said, "You have insufficient funds."

"Insufficient funds?" I exclaimed.

"You have no money!"

Why didn't he just say that? "I have no money . . . that's impossible!"

"That's what they all say," he said.

I was upset . . . no . . . I would have to say that I went right past upset and on to INDIGNANT! The situation was an embarrassment!

"Look again!" I said. After all, assuming that the bank did lose track of my money, why should the teller doubt me?

I told him that my account was *not* insufficient of funds. "I opened an account with your bank with my paychecks. I worked hard for that money! I know that I have money! You made a BIG mistake!"

I was about to fall apart and tell him that my mother wouldn't like the way he was treating me and that my dad was over six feet tall! Suddenly and very pompously, that teller person asked, "Do you have your receipt?"

"Receipt! You made the error! Why should I be put in the position of defending my balance?" Those were logical arguments, but no one ever said that businesspersons were allowed the luxury of trusting everyman.

OOPS. I knew that Mom was out as a defense because after all those trips to the bank, all those charlotte russe cakes, all those stairway reminders, in my hour of need when I should have drawn upon all the resources of my receipt education, I had NOTHING! I had no leg to stand on, no excuse, no recourse, and no receipt.

I clearly remember (oh, my!) throwing mine into the trash can on the way out of the bank. I went through a series of emotions that began with surprise and ended with tears.

I asked to see the bank president. I think I got the branch manager (who also happened to have young working offspring).

The man was a saint, and he listened in total amazement (yet with a refreshed ear) to this dinosaur of the Girls' Catholic School System who was lecturing him about the fact that I had trusted him with my funds, my hard-earned money, and that now I had none! Even without a receipt there ought to be some way for him to know that I really had made a deposit that would make me solvent. The bank needed a better backup system. And why, when it came down to his word against mine, was I automatically the loser?

"Does that seem fair to you?" It didn't seem equitable to me that the loss of one little tiny receipt meant no little tiny belief! Where was my money?

Be Prepared!

Now the burden of proof was on my shoulders. The manager spent very patient moments explaining that it was not his policy or his judgment but merely the bank's rules. He let me know that I was not alone in my opinion of the stony, heartless institution; his own daughter agreed with me about his business policies.

He said that he really thought his daughter and I

ought to meet sometime because it appeared to him that we had a lot in common! Until then, he assured me that he and the bank would do everything possible to find my money, despite the fact that when there was no 25¢ charlotte russe involved, I had not saved my bank receipt.

After many years of wondering, "Why save the bank receipt?" I had my answer!

Retracing my steps on that infamous day, they discovered (I deposited money for my mom, too) I had filled out two slips for my parents' account and none for mine. We realized that my life's savings were safe in my parents' account. From that day to this, I have learned we all need to understand that we should save our receipts. "JUST BECAUSE AND JUST IN CASE!"

If you don't have your receipt, you have very little recourse, and you may not have a return when you run into a problem concerning quality, reliability, performance, need, or purpose.

> ***Save your receipts*** **just because**
> ***and*** **just in case!**

If the item in question doesn't work right all the time the way it should when you need it to do what you bought it to do, you will be able to fill in the reason when the actual need for a legitimate return arises.

Be prepared! "JUST BECAUSE AND JUST IN CASE!"

CHAPTER 4

YOU'RE NOT ALONE

THERE ARE LITERALLY A BUSHEL FULL OF REASONS (other than receiptlessness) that prevent people from RETURNING SOMETHING.

It takes too long.
It's too far.
It's not worth the gas.
I can't find the bag.
I lost the tickets.
They won't give me my money.
I can't be bothered.
I'm scared.
I'm embarrassed.

You're not alone. Embarrassment is one of the most common excuses for not taking it back—other than receiptlessness! People say they feel that they have done something wrong and they feel guilty about going back to the store.

Shopper's Awareness

Dismiss the guilt! Follow your instincts. They are usually correct. And use your new shopper's awareness!

Know your rights! Ignore your guilt, and practice return-it skills. Good returns are no accident.

Many people say, "I don't know what to say." That is normal. It's okay. Just say, "I want to return this!"

Good returns are no accident.

Try it. Practice at home. Look yourself in the mirror and say, "I want to return this!"

Prepare your conversation at home, and answer your own objections. Then when you walk up to the counter, you will be convincing when you say, "I want to return this!"

Now the weight is off your shoulders, and it's all up to the salesperson.

"That's what I was afraid of," you say.

Well, don't be afraid. *How to Return Just About Anything* is here to encourage you, to remind you that the salespersonnel are not your enemies, and to say that they will award you a medal if you show up with your receipt and your original packaging. (If they don't, we will cover that in another chapter.)

Orderly Receipts

I once encountered a salesperson who called her supervisor over to show her a customer who had her receipt in order and had labeled it. Now that doesn't sound like such an amazing thing to have simply marked "Pat's pants" on the receipt for Pat's pants. But to them it was one of the wonders of the world!

She said that she wished more people would have their returns in order because it was so much easier to process the exchange or credit. She said that people often think the salespersons do not want to help, but they are there to serve you and they want to make things as easy as possible for everyone. However, they have certain procedures that they must follow. Their jobs depend on it. She went on to say that you wouldn't believe some of the things they see.

The obvious would include no receipt and a bad attitude. People become rude because they are worried about losing their money. That is a real concern, but it is not the salesperson's fault. We would never do that. We're prepared return-it people.

The not so obvious would include a broken vase. The customer felt that the vase shouldn't have broken so easily (she only dropped it once!).

There were ripped seams on a woman's favorite dress. "It fit when I bought it!" she cried. The dress was size fourteen, and the woman was rapidly bursting out of a size sixteen!

A man's suit was out of style. The gentleman said, "I would like to exchange this." (The suit had wide lapels. Narrow lapels were in.) An entire "style cycle change" is too long a time frame to expect an exchange or return on an item like this. Warranty or guarantee situations would be circumstances that might alter the situation.

The moral of the story is, the salespersonnel of the world are more afraid of what the public may unleash upon them in a return situation than you could ever be afraid of returning under justified situations.

Justified situations—those times when you know in your heart that you honestly have a right to return. A situation where you honestly feel that you have not gotten your money's worth. A true problem with size, quantity, fit, insurance, warranties, defects, contracts, theft, verification, quality, or identification that causes you to be dissatisfied.

A situation where you know in your heart and conscience that you are entitled to satisfaction for a poor sale. A situation where you will be exercising your right to return in order to correct an error or a problem with the product.

A True Return-It Situation

A true return-it situation requires an honest complaint—one where we are not trying to get something for nothing but one where we are trying to protect the quality, the reliability, the performance, the need, the purpose, of the purchase by returning it.

Reward your salesperson with a wonderful workday of selling and refunding, and reward yourself with a wonderful day of buying and returning, by practicing in an ethical manner your return-it skills.

A true return-it situation requires an honest complaint.

As the sales supervisor said, "A receipt and the original packaging make my life easy!" A receipt and the original packaging make your life return-it easy!

CHAPTER 5

I-SIMPLY-CHANGED-MY-MIND THEORY

We all must learn to give ourselves the benefit of the I-Simply-Changed-My-Mind Theory.

This theory means that it doesn't have to be broken, that it doesn't have to "not fit," that it doesn't have to be the wrong color, that it doesn't have to be dented for you to ask for the money you spent back!

Return-it has to do with the right to simply do it!

Even if there is nothing wrong?

Yes! You can return even if there is nothing wrong.

"It's Just Not Right!"

When you return an article and the salesperson asks, "Reason for return?" you may say, "I simply changed my mind!"

> *You can return even if there is nothing wrong.*

You do not need a reason for a timely return if you have protected your right (kept your receipt) and if you are returning the item under all the conditions of the store's policies. In thinking about it, most people have sound reasons for their returns, but they just can*not* put their fingers on the exact reason why they are not happy with the purchase.

"It's just not right!"

"It could be better."

"It's a little too . . ."

"I guess it will do (even if you don't know what it is)."

Reputable stores have provided you with the right to say—even if you don't quite know why—"I simply changed my mind!"

No Guilt

You can learn to do it all without guilt.

Returning is a learned behavior but something you are very seldom taught to do effectively. There are volumes written on how to shop, how to get a great buy, how to get the most for your money, but virtually nothing has been written to offer help on how to return just about anything until now.

Responsible Returns

I love the fact that I have the right to return. I never abuse it . . . I use it. I protect it by being a responsible return-it person.

Returning is a learned behavior.

I learned a lot about shopping by having the comfort of knowing that I can correct most buying mistakes that I might make along the way!

CHAPTER 6

HOW TO GET THE JOB DONE

WE HAVE OUR PHILOSOPHY. NOW LET'S GET TO SOME RETURN-IT METHODS!

As we progress through this "How to Get the Job Done" chapter, we will continue to examine more of the age-old excuses for keeping White Elephants. One of the classic excuses that people use to get themselves off "the return-it hook" is "I don't have time!" (subtitled) "It isn't worth it!" to run all over the earth to return one little item.

You are absolutely right. Running all over the earth is not a part of my return-it philosophy. But you do have the time to return on an organized route.

It will put money back in your pocket for the purchases you really do need and keep White Elephants out of your backyard! That is true in every case because most of your returning is done on roads and in places where you are going to be going anyway. You are going to be in or going by most of the places that would be on your return route, whether or not you are planning to return anything.

"To return" or "not to return" is really only a decision of "Yes, I will!" or "Not right now!" if you are prepared for the event in the event that you do want to return it.

Get Organized

First, get a return-it container. If you own a car, get a box, cube, bin, sack, or anything of a secure nature to use for your return-it container. Put it in your car or van and leave it there.

If you are a public transportation person, get a sturdy canvas bag with a strong handle or strap. Let all members in the household know where it is so they can put it to good return-it use!

In the cube or bag, place a tiny bag or box with a permanent marker, a package of stick-on labels, tape, and a stapler. You will use these every time that you have a return. Put the return in its original packaging and then in the bag that the store gave you to bring the item home.

Put your receipt in the bag. Staple it closed. Stick a label on the bag and mark it "Jenny's jeans, credit card used, and store name."

If you do not want to put your receipt in the bag, you can label the bag and leave the receipt in the holder that you used to file it when you purchased the item. If your return doesn't require a bag, tape the information to the original packaging. Now put the bag in your return cube or travel sack. Just like expectant parents, you will have a bag packed and ready!

If you have your returnable item in your return cube in your car or travel bag, you are prepared to make a return at any moment or at a moment's notice when you happen to be at the store or, better yet, on a planned route.

You're ready when you have a "just because" it didn't fit, it's too big, it's okay but not great occasion to return or a "just in case" occurrence or a "HMMMM . . . that's it!" says your wife occurrence to return it.

Get a receipt holder. It's your mobile file. You take it everywhere.

I use a credit card holder, but a little zipper bag, cosmetic case, pencil holder case, box, pouch, or tiny purse will do the job fine!

I like the credit card holder; it seems to be efficient for me. But if you are more comfortable with a different system for your receipts, do what works best for you. Always be certain that you follow your system faithfully.

Then when you have a return (with my system), you will go to your receipt folder, and under, in the compartment next to, in the compartment above, or in the same compartment, you will find the credit card that you used for the purchase and the receipt that you need for the return. I always like to put the receipt under the credit card in the same compartment, but it is up to you to decide what works best for you.

Follow your system faithfully.

You will find the receipt in the compartment because you put it there immediately after you signed it and heard the salesperson say, "Have a good day!"

The salespersonnel usually put the receipt in the bag, but you must learn to ask for the receipt! Once that little piece of validation, your proof of purchase, your guarantee of satisfaction, finds its way into the bag, there is no way to know where it could wind up.

Receipts that go into bags remind me of the last piece of cake in a house full of kids and the change in your purse on the day before payday. When you need them and when you go to get them, they're never there!

When you are ready to pay for an item while you are shopping, have your receipt holder out, open it to your credit card, take out the card, and leave the holder open in your hand. Rest the receipt on the holder as you sign the credit card slip. Have a pen ready or use the same pen that the salesperson gave you to sign the credit slip, and mark the receipt on the back "credit card name, Scott's shoes, and Wally's Department Store."

Fold the receipt and slip it back into the card holder while you put your credit card away. Put it under the card, in the same slot, or in another slot near the card.

This method keeps your receipt and your credit card

immediately at hand. Do not feel that you should not take the time to write this information on the receipt. It is your receipt! If the store has the right to ask you to stand at the register and fill out information that it needs for the record of the sale, then don't you think that you have the right to take a minute to write some important information on your receipt so that if the "JUST IN CASE" or the "JUST BECAUSE" happens, you will have all the information that you will need to make a return?

The little bit of time that it will take to put your receipt in a safe place will be your return insurance policy. When a store says, "Satisfaction guaranteed," the promise has a note of reserve—"providing that you have a receipt!"

Your System Pays Off

Now you must take a minute to realize, too, that even the best systems occasionally develop a snag, and there may be times when you have to defend your rights rather than merely exercise them even when you have your receipt. Haven't there been times when you have made a return with a receipt and the person handling the return scrutinized the receipt, questioned the information, required more identification, called for a supervisor and, generally speaking, made you uncomfortable for no legitimate reason? You should then realize how important your few minutes of informational note taking on your receipt may be to your "satisfaction guaranteed" and how important that little bit of proof in your receipt holder will be to returning just about anything.

If the saleswoman says, "You did not buy this item in this department," you will have your receipt that says "Jenny's jeans" (Jenny is seven). You will be able to say, "I bought these jeans for my daughter from the children's department," instead of fumbling around in your wallet or at the bottom of your pockets looking for your receipt.

If your receipt should fall out of your bag, if your receipt should get ripped off your bag, do you think that the store will accept these two "ifs" that happened as valid reasons to return an item without a receipt? If the "JUST IN CASE" occurs with one of your purchases? If the blade breaks off your blender? If the seat sags in your new slacks? If the wallpaper falls off the wall? If the new headphones don't fit your head? If the slats fall out of the bed? If the red shirt is pink after the final rinse?

In all my return-it experience I have never heard anyone tell me a return-it story that began with, "Once upon a time my receipt fell out of the bag, but the store clerk didn't mind!" or "Once upon a time . . . my receipt got torn off the bag (after it was stapled to the package), but the store clerk said, 'We're sorry about that. Here is your money!'"

Accept the fact that out in the shopping world, even though reputable stores have fine return policies, you are (nevertheless) guilty until proven innocent!

It is a cold, hard fact, but it supports the Charlotte Russe Theory: no proof equals no identity! As my banker said, "It's not my policy, but . . ." Be prepared because even though we would like to think "it" won't happen to us, the "what" we would like to think won't happen to us will happen!

I know because every time I thought that "it"—a product defect, two of the same things, Grandpa hated the shirt, Aunt Susie won't like "that," "I *can't* wear those, Mom!" or "I gave those up!"—would never happen to me, "it" happened!

Give yourself the benefit of the doubt, and you will be pleasantly surprised to find your receipt will be where you put it when you need it.

Advantage of Credit Cards

The ideal situation for returning occurs when you have given yourself every advantage by using credit cards. As you can see by the nature of this book, I do not stress credit cards to be used for anything other than what you were going to buy with cash. I do not suggest using them to buy items that you were not already planning to buy.

Impulse buying often leads to "the need to return" because you didn't need it in the first place! I merely recommend that you put the cash in your bank, earn interest on your money, and pay your bill in full when you receive your statement and bill from the credit card company or store.

With this method, you have completed a "normal checkout" and prepared yourself (at the same time) to do a "normal return" as a confident return-it shopper "when" and "if" you need to do one. "JUST BECAUSE AND JUST IN CASE!"

If for some reason you are not paying with a credit card, this method will still work perfectly. You will simply put the receipt in an empty slot in the credit card folder after you have marked on the back "Scott's shoes, Wally's Department Store, cash," or "Scott's shoes, Wally's Department Store, check #0000."

If you are a "cash only" person, the method is the same, but you will use your credit card folder as a receipt only folder. We will discuss the cash flow problems that can arise with real live money. As long as you are aware of potential difficulties you can make the "cash" or "card" decision when you are preparing for your shopping trip.

> *Impulse buying often leads to "the need to return" because you didn't need it in the first place.*

When I was learning the shopping rudiments back in Bayonne, New Jersey, checks were a method of payment totally unheard of and unacceptable. In those days when you shopped, you went with cash. If you tried to pay for a purchase with a check, it was assumed that you really didn't have any money.

"Will You Take a Check?"

I remember being totally involved in eavesdropping as I overheard a customer in a hosiery shop having a conversation with the saleswoman. The customer had planned to purchase several pairs of stockings, which in those days was no small task because all the hosiery was displayed in individual boxes. You were assigned a saleswoman who showed you pair after pair by taking them out of the counter and pulling one of each pair up on her arm so that the customer could see the color. It was work and could be expensive because if she snagged the stocking, she owned the pair. Consequently, when the customer decided on her selection and then discovered that she didn't have enough money, it was a seriously embarrassing moment! However, that didn't cause nearly the turmoil that her next question stirred: "Will you take a check?"

The saleswoman gasped and nearly swooned into a faint, but instead she gathered herself up from her close encounter with the floor and hollered in a "shrill whisper," "Manager . . . Manager!"

Then she began to fan herself with the hosiery box cover until she spotted her bell! In all the excitement she had forgotten that that was the method of choice for signaling the manager. The saleswomen were required to call him to approve their addition on the sales slip tally before they finalized the sale.

She grabbed the bell and jingled it fiercely until the manager arrived.

"What's the problem here? What's the problem here?" he sputtered and stuttered.

"This woman hasn't got enough money to pay for her stockings," the saleswoman whispered in a very soft voice. Then she boomed all over the store, "SHE WANTS TO PAY FOR THEM WITH A CHECK!"

All the people in the shop stopped what they were doing! "Ohhhhs" and "nnoooooos" were heard everywhere!

I never did learn the outcome of the sale because my mom was finished, and we couldn't find a graceful way to stay and eavesdrop any longer.

After that check experience, it was strange to me as the years flew by that people were routinely paying for things with checks without even asking for permission.

Now the standard question asked by the salesforces of the world is, "Cash, check, or charge!" They say it with an exclamation point in their voices because there is no doubt about, no question about, no suspicion concerning the use of any of the methods of payment.

Time flies when you're shopping. Things change when you least expect them to!

What wasn't is. What was unthinkable is commonplace.

But therein lies the only hidden catch of paying by check. On the return side of the sale the stores feel that if they are willing to trust you "out the door" with their merchandise on the merit of your check and its identification, you must be willing to wait approximately two weeks, sometimes as long as a month, for a refund check to be mailed. Therefore, to protect your cash flow, you must be aware of this time frame for check returns, especially on big-ticket items.

Same-Day Returns

If you purchase something by check and you find that you can*not* use it and you need the money immediately to purchase a replacement item, return it immediately! This is the only time I advise same-day returns because they usually are not necessary or convenient.

Nevertheless in this case, if you get back to the store before the salesclerks change the money drawer, they will usually void the sale, take back the merchandise, give back your check, and thank you for shopping at Wally's!

To ensure that you get to the check before the office persons put it into the bank envelope, you can call the business office or the department where you made the purchase and ask them to hold the check. Tell them that you are coming back to the store within the hour to return the merchandise. Calling the department where you purchased the item is usually the fastest way to handle the transaction; however, the department personnel do not always have the authority to handle this type of return. In that case, ask to speak to the supervisor of the department or to be connected to the business office.

If you do not beat the clock, be prepared to wait. This "hurry up and wait" hold on check returns will apply until fourteen working days have passed. By then the store policy makers feel that the check has cleared the bank, and therefore, they will not mind giving you cash for the item returned because they know that they have received money from the bank for the item in question. Prior to that time they know that if they pay you for a return before the check has cleared and it doesn't clear, the store has lost money. Read the store's time frame for returns, especially with checks.

Some of the smaller stores have a seven-day cash or credit return policy. If you wait until you can return the item and get your money (all in one trip, the recommended way when there are no time restrictions), you may risk your refund because the seven-day period has expired—even though the store set the rule for the fourteen-day waiting period on check purchases.

Always read the sign stating the return policies for each store. No matter where you shop, no matter what you are buying, if you do not see the policies posted, ask to see them! If you do not agree with the return policies, shop elsewhere.

For your own protection always be able to walk away from a store with a poor return policy. Believe it or not, there will always be another one, a perfect one, the "only" one SOMEWHERE ELSE!

Always read the sign stating the return policies for each store.

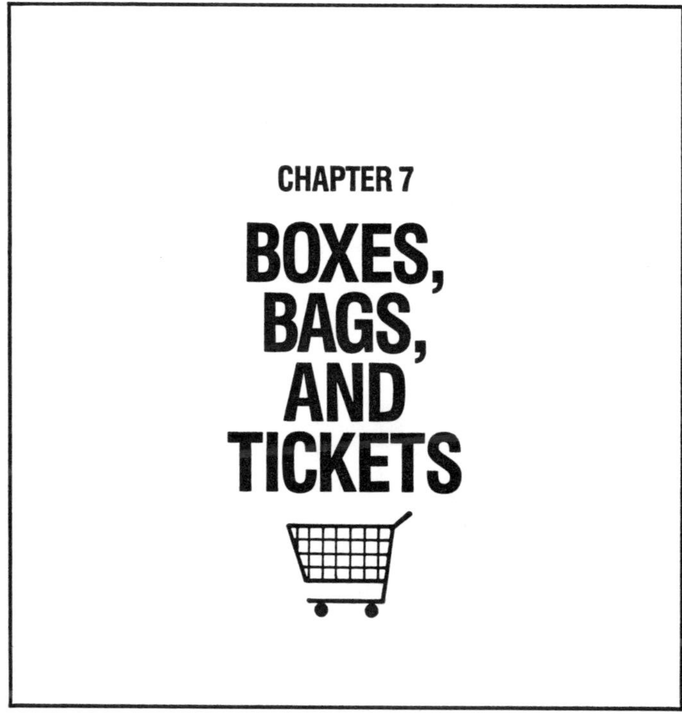

CHAPTER 7

BOXES, BAGS, AND TICKETS

SAVE YOUR ORIGINAL PACKAGING.

The boxes, the bags, and the tickets do not go in the trash! Most returns on new items require original packaging, and quality control problems usually require original packaging, even if a period of time has passed before a problem becomes apparent.

> *Most returns on new items require original packaging.*

Store It

Store your original packaging. Keep the box that the

power drill,
baby doll,
paint set,
miniblinds,
baby stroller,
sewing machine,
hair dryer,
arcade game,
silverware,
computer,
suit,
or
boots came in!

From your birthday, Christmas, special occasion, or no special occasion, flatten boxes and save them.

Store the original packaging on a garage shelf, under a bed, in a closet, behind a bookcase, down in the basement, up in the attic, over at your dad's (if he has more room), at the office, behind the dresser, around the corner (at a neighbor's).

Save Bags

Save the store bags. On a hanger or hook somewhere in your house, designate the "bagger" hook. Hang a bag of some sort to be used to save all the store bags from the various department and specialty stores where you shop. Always keep an assortment of sizes and stores to use for returns in case your original bag gets ripped or too rumpled to be useful or presentable.

Then when the "just because" or the "just in case" happens, you can get the item, put it back into its original packaging, pull out a store bag, put the return in the bag with your receipt (if you wish), staple the bag, put it into your cube or travel bag, label it with the store, item, credit card, and return it!

CHAPTER 8

RESPONSIBILITY IN THE PRICE TAG

One morning I got a call from one of my dearest friends. We have compared notes and conferred with each other through years of children, holidays, trends, moves, trivia games, wallpaper selections, and purchases! All of which we have savored over hundreds of cups of coffee.

Our boys had gotten remote control vehicles for Christmas, and we were discussing the expense involved and their vulnerability. Santa had decided to bring the do-it-yourself remote control vehicles because he knew that if the toys crashed at the hands of the boys (or the real little kids . . . the dads), they could be repaired, parts could be replaced, and even though it was quite a task to assemble the kits, they were great quality time projects for the boys, old and young, together!

Carol said, "I'm really disappointed in the boat we got. It's a piece of junk!"

"Really? What's the matter with it?" I asked.

"Well, it's a hydroplane, and the rubber tube is all cracked!"

"Why don't you take it back?"

"Well, we bought it in November, and now it's April! We had to get it early for Christmas to be sure that Santa would have one ready to put in his sack. You remember how popular they were!" she said. "Do you think they will take it back after all this time?"

"They ought to," I replied.

"It was expensive enough! And we had to buy batteries and a quick charger, too!"

Yup! Carol was bitten. She was becoming more and more convinced.

"You are right!" she said. "I paid a lot of money for that thing!"

With firmness and resolve in her voice she said, "I'm going to take it back."

The next morning the phone rang, and a voice answered my "hello" with, "I'm nervous! What should I say?"

"First . . . don't be nervous. You are right! You did spend a lot of money—more than $200—on a toy. Don't you think that there is a responsibility in that price tag for the store and the manufacturer to provide quality?"

"But . . . what if it was our fault?" said Carol.

"How could it be your fault?"

"Well . . . we ran it in the pool."

"Where else would you run a toy boat other than a contained area? You wouldn't want to run an expensive toy in a wide open place . . . where a slip of the controls could set the Merry Christmas gift of the year out to sea on a long voyage . . . a $200 bon voyage."

"What should I say?" asked Carol.

"Say as little as possible. Simply go to the toy store with your return item, smile, and say, 'I want to return this!' Calmly place the boat on the counter and hand the receipt to the person at the desk."

"Really? Don't I need to tell them why?"

"Yes, but not until they ask! They may not question the reason. Your receipt may be all they want . . . the proof of purchase. If they want more information, they will ask for it."

"Well, I certainly have my proof. I have my receipts for the boat, the charger, and the batteries, and I've already put them in their original boxes! They are in the toy store bag. What else do I need?"

"You've got it all. . . . NOW, just return it!"

A Return-It Success Story

She did. With shaky knees and a determined will, she walked in, quietly set the boat on the counter, and said the magic words, "I want to return this boat!"

The saleswoman looked at the receipt and said, "You have had this boat awhile. It has been an awfully long time."

Carol replied in the briefest form, "We bought this toy for Christmas, and now the rubber tube is cracking."

"But it has been five months," said the woman. "I'll get the manager."

Carol remained calm. *After all, this is a normal procedure,* she thought to herself. *If I were the saleswoman, I would get the manager, too.*

He came over, looked at the date on the receipt, whispered some return talk in the saleswoman's ear, gave Carol a few glances from her to the receipt, from her to the receipt again—looks that were meant to see if she was serious about the return.

He finally broke the silence and said, "You've had this awhile."

Carol replied, "I should expect to have it quite awhile because it was a very expensive toy! The rubber cracked in five months, and I would have expected it to last for years!"

"You're right!" He refunded the money for the boat, the batteries, and the charger.

The following morning Carol's success brewed up a Return-It Cup of Coffee Celebration! Not because the store would have done any less but because Carol knew her rights and exercised them. The toy store manager knew she was right, and he honored "satisfaction guaranteed policy"!

You need not settle for any less when you are a prepared return-it person. What else could any return-it person ask for?

Nothing, except the actual return of the money to your pocket, credit to your account, or check to your mailing address.

But wait. Our coffee cup is only half full. Our celebration is timely but a little premature until we actually get the money!

Return Credit Slips

At the store pay close attention to the return credit slip. Make certain that you have the salesperson staple it to your original receipt. This credit to your account, this credit to refund check #0000, which will be sent to your mailing address, can be validated only by the new credit slip that you received for the proof of your return.

When the salesperson asks, "Do you want the old receipt?" you say, "Yes!" Always take your old receipt.

At the store pay close attention to the return credit slip.

"Why must I keep both receipts?" you ask. If you do not keep the receipt that credited the return to your account, how will you prove that you ever returned the item in case it does not appear on your credit card statement at the end of the billing period? *Then,* in the event that the store accidentally fails to credit your return, you have the original receipt to show that you purchased the item, returned it and, according to your credit card statement, received no credit for the return!

If you do not ask for the original receipt, you can also have a problem if you need to return other items on the same receipt. File all your returned receipts with your credit card receipts in a little pouch, envelope, box, folder, or whatever type of file suits your bookkeeping needs. Even a drawer will do as long as you consistently file.

It doesn't matter what kind of holder you actually

use. The grandmas of the world have been known to save millions under their mattresses! Not a conventional bank but very efficient!

File all your returned receipts with your credit card receipts.

Check Your Statement

At the end of each month or whenever you do your bills, grab your pouch, and check your statements. Look for

4/28/XX toy store

—$200 Boat
— 59 Charger
— 28 Batteries

If the statement fails to show the return, it could be that the billing period closed before the store credited the return to your account and that it will appear next month; that somehow the credit never reached the credit card company; that the salesperson did the return incorrectly.

You pick up on all these possibilities immediately because you have a file with your returns that you check religiously until they appear on your statement as money back in your pocket.

If they do not appear or they appear incorrectly, call your account representative for your credit card company. The telephone number for the "Questions About Your Account" is usually found in the informational section of the statement in tiny print at the very bottom of the statement with a 1-800 number offering twenty-four-hour account service. How can you miss?

You have grand return-it skills and a large institution to help with your "Receipt Return Tracking" and the ability to put the return into a "Dispute" through the credit card company if you have trouble returning the item or getting credit for the return. All this is possible because you kept your receipts and kept track of your "Credited to Your Account" entries on your credit card statements.

Wouldn't you say that it was worth the effort, and there was very little running around involved? The easiest way to return efficiently is to return on a planned route. The boat return had very little running around, especially since it was so well organized, but we can perfect this method by having a return-it day at the mall!

When you have a return cube in the car or (if you are a walker) a return travel bag hanging nearby, on a return-it day you drive your car or grab your bag and walk to the bus, to the subway, to the train.

Have lunch with a friend.

See a movie at the mall.

AND RETURN IT!

CHAPTER 9

THE ORGANIZED RETURN ROUTE

IT IS WORTH IT.

I'll give you an example of a normal return-it day on an organized route. A normal return-it day is every day. Can you think of a day in your life when you didn't buy something on your own shopper power or through the purchasing power of someone else? Of course not! Even as a baby, you were buying with someone, for someone, or going along for the ride with a friend.

We all can remember the endless hours of running to the grocery store, the repair place, the hardware store, the bakery, and the butcher.

We all can remember times when a friend's mom would pick us up to play and we would go through a long list of

"I gotta stop here awhile."

"Just let me run in here a minute."

"Oops we need some milk."

"I'll run in really fast!"

"Dad's dry cleaning should be ready."

"Just a second more!"

"This is absolutely the last stop."

By the time we arrived to play, Mom had called to say she's on her way to do some errands and pick us up!

Think of all the bored husbands on the benches of the malls dealing with the everyday necessity of being there shopping.

Shopping is an every day affair. We buy and return every day! Simply remind yourself that for every shopping day, there is a normal return-it day.

A Busy Return-It Day

These items were exchanged or returned in one day:

2 Iced tea makers (each) $34.95
extra pots (free)

Little green dress
socks $ 4.95

Ninja Turtle watch
(exchange)

Stove saucers $10.00

I had shopped early for my younger son's birthday present because he wanted a Ninja Turtle watch. His birthday was Tuesday, and on the Saturday before, my older son saw it and said, "He wanted a blue band!"

OOPS! I shopped with his favorite character in mind!

"Blue is his favorite color, Mom! I know he wants blue!"

Now that we had a watch to exchange, I checked my schedule and decided that Sunday would be a great return-it day! I planned the return route for Sunday afternoon while I had a baby-sitter (Dad) to occupy the Birthday Boy.

I had two iced tea makers for one store and a pair of little socks for another. Recently, I had purchased some guaranteed-to-fit stove saucers that didn't fit. I could return them on my way to put a deposit on the birthday cake. Everything was in the cube in my car. I was ready to go! Hmmmm . . . maybe I should stop at a store that is a little out of my way and return a birthday gift I had received?

My birthday was in April, and it was June 3! I was in no hurry to return the gift until it was convenient for me because I knew it would be a store credit or an exchange. Consequently, I decided to wait to return and exchange until I was in the neighborhood of the return anyway.

I had opted for the Quiet Exchange (yes, even I take the store credit occasionally!) because I knew that my friend had purchased my gift at a lovely little specialty shop owned by another very special friend of hers. She wanted to support her friend's business, and so did I! Nevertheless, I usually do not recommend this approach because you could lose buying power.

How can that happen? And why? Time can be your enemy in a "no receipt exchange" because unless you wish to exchange item for item (which you usually do not do), you have only a fifty-fifty chance of finding what you received in the color or size that you do want! The items could have gone on sale or even on clearance.

If you do not "buy" the same item that you are returning, you are forced to buy something that is not the original value of the gift but the value of the item as it is priced on sale or on clearance.

> ***Time can be your enemy in a "no receipt exchange."***

You are forced to accept the sale or clearance value of the item. You might have been given a $50 gift, and you could wind up taking a gift worth $25 and even less if clearance is slashed off after the 50 percent sale! I gambled with my gift because I knew that I could always ask for the receipt (if need be); I would just have preferred not to do it! (It was my choice.)

But I want you to know your choices and then to act according to your wishes. At the moment it was my wish not to get that far off the beaten path.

I wanted to travel an efficient route and to avoid extra traffic. Generally speaking, I start my return routes after a leisurely breakfast with a good friend at a favorite breakfast place. I arrive at the mall as the doors are opening. The ideal time is what is the best time for your schedule. It takes a little time to plan a route, but you waste a lot of time and money if you do not "plan" to return.

We do not "just return." We "plan" to return. We are beginning to see that planning to return means more than just planning to do it someday . . . maybe?

The cube is packed. The route is planned. Everyone understands that we plan to actually return it now!

We do not "just return." We "plan" to return.

We are at the mall. Grab your little map!

Oh, yes, a little sketched map of your mall with the alleys and aisles marked always saves you endless footsteps and may provide you with a little leftover time to have a cup of your favorite flavored coffee at the food court. The mall map is a perfect little fun project for your kids on a rainy day. If you laminate it, you can slip it into your wallet or bag. Very often the mall supplies a map (at no cost) at the main Customer Service Center. These booths are usually located near the center of the mall not far from the main escalator or elevator. While other people are still looking for the big directory in the mall somewhere, you will already be there! Hint: your children can laminate it with tape from your return cube necessity tool box.

I returned the socks, exchanged the watch, and

bought the iced tea maker. Wait a minute. Didn't I say that I was returning two iced tea makers? That's right, but first I had to buy one more to return two.

I actually wanted to keep one of the two that I was returning, but I couldn't get a credit adjustment on the maker that I wanted to keep because the ten-day sale adjustment period had ended. The only way that I could get the sale price would be to take them both back and then buy another one. I did that!

Originally, I had purchased two makers as gifts . . .

2 at a sale price (each) of	$34.95
2 free pitchers ($7.95)	$00.00
(1 extra for each)	
	$69.90
plus tax	$ 4.19

Then one afternoon in the car pool line a friend told me that she heard (from a saleswoman) that the iced tea maker would be on sale this weekend for $29.95 without the free pitcher (valued at $7.95).

My dad had plenty of pitchers at home to store extra tea so I returned the one for $34.95, and I bought it again for $29.95!

A free pitcher is great, but a better sale price is greater! I had to return it and buy it again because the ten-day sale adjustment period was over, but the right to return it was still mine. Then I returned the other one that I had purchased for a shower gift. It turned out to be a duplicate.

I checked my map. I went around the corner and up the escalator to return the burner saucers.

Now I was ready to have my gourmet coffee: "Raspberries and cream, please!"

Let's check the list of transactions:

2 Iced tea makers (returned)	$69.90
1 Pair of socks (returned)	$ 4.95
1 Set of burner saucers (returned)	$10.00
Back-in-Pocket Total	$84.85 plus or minus tax
minus 1 Iced tea maker	−$29.95
	$54.90

And I had the satisfaction of an even return for a watch. Keep in mind by returning and buying again, I saved $5.00 more on an item I had already purchased on a trip to the mall that I planned to make!

Shopping Clues

When you are buying an item, always ask the salesperson for shopping clues. Before you pay, ask, "Has this been on sale during the last ten days?" If the answer is yes, ask for an immediate cost adjustment. If the answer is no, ask if the item will be going on sale in the next ten days.

Then make a note of the sale date on your receipt. People are conditioned to buy through sales, but we must also condition ourselves to return because of sales for credit adjustments. It may be only $5 on a teapot, but on a big item or several items in a storewide sale, it can be a sizable amount of money!

At Holidays

At holiday seasons make a special trip to the mall with a list of all the purchases made store by store. Walk through each department. Check for sales on purchases. If there are sales, request credit adjustments immediately!

When the mall is having a mallwide sale or a storewide sale, many items will be reduced from 20 percent to 60 percent of the ticketed price. Consequently, I often combine my shopping list and my mall list into a folder.

This is my busy season approach! Make a list of all your shopping needs. Make a list for each major store where you do business. Make one list for the smaller miscellaneous shops. As you make your purchases, under each store enter the gift, person, and date.

When you are shopping, you will be able to see what else you need to buy. From your store lists, you will be able to see what you have already purchased and where.

As you wander through on your mall routes, whatever the time of day your list will be ready for you to shop by. Buying or returning, with your lists you are prepared to grab a sale by returning for a store credit adjustment, returning for "satisfaction guaranteed"—all at a moment's notice!

With your receipts and your lists you will be a walking, talking, prepared, organized, personalized, return-it file!

Do not be afraid to shop by returning if you see that an item you have purchased has gone on sale. Merchandise returned after the ten-day period for adjustments should have a valid reason for return, but you should take advantage of the store's sale. In the case of the returned iced tea maker, my dad really did not need another pitcher, but as a valued customer of the store he should be rewarded with the better sale price on the item if it is unused and in the original packaging.

Customer Loyalty

I find it a little annoying that loyal regular customers who shop at their favorite stores purchase what they need when they need it and often miss sales, but an occasional shopper who is not so "store loyal" can clean up on a sale and save a lot. Do not be afraid to say, "I purchased this iced tea maker less than thirty days ago. My dad can use a better sale price more than he can use a free pitcher. . . . I would like to return this since it is too late to get a simple sale price adjustment. Then I will buy another one at the new promotional price. I have everything unopened and in its original packaging."

Reputable stores welcome your loyalty, and they want to reward their regular customers as well as their "sale" customers. This is the way for them to do it. Once again the consumer has a moral obligation to respect the store's position, merchandise, and policies. Some stores do not honor returning to rebuy, but if it is done within the thirty-day period of the purchase, they usually say, "Let's get that paperwork done right now!"

The return is necessary (rather than a mere adjustment) because many of the store records are kept according to separate promotional times and sale periods.

They do not wish to deprive you of a sale price, but they can*not*—if you purchased before the ten-day purchase period—make a simple receipt adjustment.

If you purchased within the sale adjustment period (ten days before and after the sale), they will merely credit the difference back to your account, or in the case of a cash sale, they will refund the difference in the two prices. If you purchase just prior to the sale, the store often asks you to come back with your receipt when the sale begins for your credit adjustment. Obviously, you can*not* return for a sale if you purchased the iced tea maker after the ten-day period. At that point there is no sale price, and you are out of time!

Hidden in this process is a slight problem that people who pay by check may run into. They may not be able to get a simple sale price adjustment because the check would not have cleared the bank if they purchased the item after the sale began. A check payment would almost certainly require a new purchase of the item during the sale and then a return of the first purchase when the check time period for clearing had passed. That can be done at most reputable stores as long as you return the first item within the prescribed period of time (usually thirty days after the purchase).

Always feel free to ask the salesperson if that is allowed. If the person does not know, check with a supervisor or the business office.

Once again, your list folder file can be as large as a school folder or as small as a pocket notepad. If you carry a large purse, you may prefer my file folder way. If you like to go unencumbered, you may prefer a small pocket notepad for your jacket or wallet.

A busy season approach is a wonderful tool for great shopping! Pick the method that works for you.

One of my favorite suggestions for returning in the route department is the Kids Can, Too, Theory!

Historically, one of the claims that kids have always made in this world is that they "can, too."

CHAPTER 10

THE KIDDIE ROUTE

AND THEY CAN!

Kids can see the amount of money saved in a return.

They can see that they can be discriminating shoppers who know how to buy and return.

They "can, too," shop. Kids devour the method just as they devour a pizza at their favorite restaurant.

Speaking in terms of food, we can route our kids through the mall on a school holiday, rainy day, or "boring" afternoon on a return-it treasure hunt!

If you ever announced plans to take things back to the mall on a school holiday, the children would feel

Mom and Dad had failed kiddie school procedures. But we're smarter than they think we are!

On a teacher workday when the children are home and bored, they will beg for something to do (of a non-laborious nature). They will offer a list of activities that could involve traveling one hundred miles, cost $25 in gasoline, add up to the national debt, involve fourteen friends, and/or require money for candy, a movie, and pizza (of course!).

> ***Kids can be discriminating shoppers who know how to buy and return.***

Getting Ready to Return

Be ready. Have a return route planned with one return activity for each member of your day-off crew. If older children are involved, you can let them invite a friend and return together. You should already have the items prepared in your return-it cube because with the return-it method, you prepared the item for return as soon as the need arose. You put in the original packaging, bagged it, tagged it, and cubed it!

But for the Kiddie Route, take out the selected items, unpack them, and set the labels aside. Let the kids make new labels for bags by copying the ones you had on the items (even little kids can print their labels).

Remove the items from the original packaging.

Spread the return-it treasure out in a big open space. Take the receipts out of the bags. You keep the receipts until the kids repack their items and it's time to put the receipt back in the store bag.

As you redo the return-it procedures with them, do the packing one child at a time. Start with the older children, and let them help the younger ones. When you're all ready, let each child put the bag into the return-it cube or the travel sack.

Strolling in the Mall

Returning hint: Keep a stroller in your car or garage. It is a great way to carry your return items or bring home your purchases! Use a lightweight, collapsible umbrella type that you can pick up at a garage sale.

But, you say, "We have no baby." That would be a valid argument if you could find ten strollers at the mall with babies in them!

When I used to take my babies to the mall, we would take a stroller. Before long we were carrying the baby and pushing the stroller.

I remember thinking that it wasn't much good for the baby, but it was great for packages! I even remember being foolish enough to buy a double stroller when our second baby came along. Then we were holding one, chasing one, and pushing the stroller!

When the babies grew up, I was relieved that they could walk, but I missed the stroller.

Who would ever know? I thought. *Who would ever imagine?* I mused. Everyone at the mall would be confused with a baby who used a stroller! So even though I have no baby now, I'll stroll along and pretend somehow that these packages are merely resting awhile until some baby will holler, "I WANT MY STROLLER!"

The car is ready. Examine your map—the one that you made of the mall. If you don't have one yet, that is also a wonderful activity for older children on a rainy day. Decide where you must park. Pick a starting spot at the mall. Select a meeting place for a half hour after the children have begun returning.

Tell them that they might meet with some opposition from salespersons, but if they approach the desk politely, confidently, and correctly, they should have no problems.

Should some problems arise, you will have an established time and meeting place to rally and simply go back with the young people to make the return. They will be able to see if that they run into any opposition, there is a "chain of command" to follow, and in their case it begins with you. In the meantime accompany the littlest people to do their returning.

Assuming all things go smoothly, you will all meet to compare returns, tally return dollars, plan the afternoon agenda, and allot return dollars for rainy day cost of lunch, movies, shopping, snacks, popcorn, candy, and pizza.

A Good Example

On one Kiddie Route my daughter took back a pair of volleyball shoes that weren't holding up as well as they should. Because she had her receipt, the store was authorized by the manufacturer to refund the entire amount of the original price of the shoes toward the price of a new pair of shoes. The store did not have the same shoe. It did have a better one on sale. She purchased the more expensive shoe for less than the original price of the old pair. Kristen left the store with $3.95 and a new pair of shoes!

My older son returned a video game duplication . . . $36. Scott always enjoyed a great game to play on a day off. He was happy to have money to save until he decided what he really wanted. On the ride home from our returning he took a few dollars to the video store to rent a game for several days to see if he really wanted to buy it. By the time he returned to school, he had beaten the rented game and pocketed the remaining money. He also returned a car coin holder to the men's novelty department and charged back a total of $20 to the credit card.

Jennifer and Christopher each returned an item of mine—$15 apron at the kitchen shop and $20 slippers (wrong size).

The older children can usually return items on the credit cards because the return paperwork doesn't always require a customer signature in order to be completed.

PIZZA TIME! Place your orders. Check your finances:

$ 3.95 Kristen's refund
$20.00 Scott's refund
$15.00 Christopher's total
$20.00 Jennifer's tally
$58.95 disposable income

We can*not* use the money from the arcade game since it was a gift and belonged to Scott. That is why I gave him two return items. I usually try to make sure that they are returning items that will put money back into my pocket before I rebudget it for free day activities!

Kristen had actually shopped by returning. Scott got an opportunity to try a game for a little while before he rushed out and bought one that he would have been bored with. The rest of the amount could be considered money that I would have spent on a day of entertainment anyway.

On these Kiddie Routes, I try to return items that are not needed and that I was not planning to repurchase. Then I have truly reallocated the money for a new purpose and I have not left myself with a budget deficit for school shoes because I spent the money on movies and pizza.

A Reassuring Message

You have had a fun day and a lesson in finance without spending any more than you would have spent in the first place. You will spend a good portion of the return money, but you have shown the children how dollars add up and how much a day of fun can cost.

You will be amazed and pleasantly surprised at how conscientious the children will be when they understand where the money comes from and how much it costs to shop! You can teach it all with positive reinforcement and a fun Kiddie Route Day!

They get a message that their efforts are appreciated, their choices are approved, and their mistakes are correctable.

In a real life learning situation, they can be capable, considerate, educated "Can, Too, Kids"!

CHAPTER 11

A COUPLE OF BUCKS ADD UP!

Let's discuss some of the other deterrents in that bushel full of excuses for not practicing return-it skills!

You do it! (Laziness!)
I've had it too long!
They won't take it back now!
They won't take "mine" back!
It's special ordered!
It's custom for me!
They don't care! (But you should.)
I might be able to use it! (Sometime?)
They won't have what I want!

I might as well keep this one!

It's only a couple of bucks.

Is it really only a couple of bucks? Let's examine this issue! We can call this discussion "a couple of bucks add up!"

Linen and the Look

I recently bought a jacket of 100 percent linen . . . 100 percent? Oops! I had broken one of my cardinal rules of dress. Linen has been and always will be on the list of I'm not neat enough to wear it.

The reason? I wrinkle enough on my own!

But we were to go to a party on New Year's Eve. The jacket was yellow (one of my better colors). It hid a multitude of sins (that were apparent in the hip area). It was perfect! At least I thought it was!

The jacket looked great, and after all at my age surely I would no longer be a victim of the World of Wrinkledom!

The World of Wrinkledom—the place where all old cotton, old linen, and other wrinkly type materials came from. All the residents of Wrinkledom own stock in iron and ironing board companies, and it was to their economic advantage to keep the population in a permanent state of wrinkles, creases, and messy twists.

The days of wrinkled shirts, ratty looking skirts, sagging blazers, baggy pants, twisted hose, crushed crinoline, mushed shirt cuffs, and bent, twisted shirtsleeves wouldn't be a part of my life again! Would they?

I had trouble all my life trying to stay neat throughout an entire day. As a teenager, I used to dream of taking a field trip with my all girls' school in conjunction with the all boys' school to the art museum in New York and returning home that evening with a romantic weekend date as a result of looking perfectly pressed.

I always returned twice as wrinkled as my "perfectly pressed" classmate who sat next to me on the bus trip. Her blonde hair would blow in the breeze from the open school bus window, and it glistened as the last sunbeams bounced off her lovely locks. My hairdo had wilted!

My mother said my "dateless state" had nothing to do with wrinkles or sunbeams but everything to do with the crimps that she and my dad put into my social schedule until they felt I was old enough to be popular!

She insisted that the Little Lovely's popularity was due not to her wrinkleless state but to the amount of freedom her parents gave her to come and go in her totally unwrinkled state. I always felt that Mom's explanation was a mother's love for a daughter. Mom insisted, however, that the date situation would take care of itself when the time was right.

Shortly after, a scientific discovery changed the direction of the fashion world—polyester! Suddenly, I knew the time was *now!* I'll admit that polyester was shiny and positively too perfect, but I LOVED IT!

My first real romance occurred on my next trip to the art museum, and my wrinkle theory was validated forever in my mind. I was also sixteen with permission to go on a date.

Which came first? Age or the Age of Polyester? Whatever . . . you can see when cotton made its return as the Fabric of the Eighties, it was very hard for me to accept.

I adjusted, but "the cotton" wrinkle was all the wrinkling that my feminine ego could take!

If my nails were polished, my hair tied with a lovely ribbon, I could finally reembrace cotton but never 100 percent linen. There was a clothing rule limit!

Me? Old-Fashioned? Never!

Wait. I must be flexible. I must guard against becoming old-fashioned.

Old-fashioned—a condition that could be epitomized by my memory of a lovely older woman who rode the bus with me on my way to school. She seemed seventy because in the era of pantyhose and no seams she still wore perfectly straight black-seamed stockings with suede open-toed shoes. Her hair was beautiful but gathered into a 1940 "do" while her cheeks were rosy and glowing with perfectly round circles of blush!

Certainly, you can see now that I had a perfectly good, sound, logical, and firmly-based-in-emotion reason for buying a linen jacket.

Just as my No Wrinkle Theory was the start of my social life, my Old-Fashioned Theory is the beginning of my flexible mental state of mind—thinking young and modern, keeping up with the trends, knowing what is "in" and "out" in my middle years!

You can also appreciate the fact that after I had some time to examine my purchase and its fabric care label, I said, "Enough of this emotional rubbish! Return it!"

You must also realize that the salesperson was very happy to have me walk in with my receipt marked Pat's jacket and the original packaging, and fill in the blank marked "Reason for Return" by simply saying, "I changed my mind!"

What's the Tally?

Now I'll show you how a couple of bucks do add up at the return register. On the linen jacket return the tally was $148 plus tax!

$ 94	JACKET
$ 30	JEWELRY
$ 24	HAIR ACCESSORIES
$148	

Return the jacket *and* the accessories. They add up, too!

Oh, yes. Once I had decided to return the jacket, I put the jacket in its box, put the receipt in the box, put the box in the bag, stapled the bag, and marked it "Pat's jacket" with the name of the store and credit card I used to purchase the items. That makes the return a speedy one if I should have a minute while I'm at the mall. I can grab the bag and make the return while I'm running to the store where I purchased the item, or it is ready and waiting for me when I make a return route trip. Then without any hesitation, I took the earrings, ribbons, and little accessories that I bought to complete the outfit, put them into their tissue paper, placed them in the bags, put the receipts in the bags, stapled the bags, and marked the bags "Pat's jewelry, Wally's Department Store, and the credit card."

Then I put the bags in the cube in the car, and without any effort it's only a couple of bucks changed to $148 saved!

> ***Little items add up to big expenses if they do not suit your needs.***

Maybe I'll decide to keep the earrings even though I don't want to keep the jacket. I put them in the cube anyway! That way they are tucked safely away with their receipt while I am deciding. In my experience, when I put the questionable items in the return-it cube, they almost always go back. If I leave the items out for the "to be or not to be decision," I wind up with a White Elephant item that I use once or twice and then wish that I had taken back.

Save a Bundle

You can save a bundle every year by simply taking back little items. Little items add up to big expenses if they do not suit your needs and—just because they were small—you did not bother to return them.

Little items turn into baby elephants that will grow to seem like big elephants because you didn't return them in a timely fashion and now you must live with them forever! I spent $94 on the jacket and $54 on the accessories. The little goodies were more than half the price of the jacket! Once again you can see why filling in "Reason for Return" only demands the simple replay:

"I want to return this because I changed my mind!"

Many people are afraid to bother anyone with a little amount when they have tiny items to return, but you can see that tiny items do add up! I couldn't quite express why I wanted to return the yellow jacket, but I had very complex, deep-rooted, and profound reasons that would actually sound quite unbalanced if I had tried to explain them!

It is perfect "returning etiquette" to say, "I simply changed my mind."

Fortunately, salespersons do not want to hear psychological ramblings on the qualities of cotton or linen and their direct effects on your life. They really do not want your life's history in the spot marked "Reason for Return." They merely want a simple statement to document the return and to present to their supervisors with their register receipts to explain their final daily balances. Naturally, they need a reason for defective products, but those reasons are easy to explain. The reasons that qualify as psychological essays are the kind that are hard to fit on those tiny lines marked, "Reason for Return."

In the gray area of "I don't know," it is perfect "returning etiquette" to say, "I simply changed my mind!"

CHAPTER 12

A QUIET EXCHANGE

MAYBE IT WILL FIT SOMEONE is on the continuing list of excuses that people give for housing White Elephants.

Maybe Mom can use it! I'll save it for Susie for college! (Susie is two.) It doesn't hurt to have two! (This excuse implies that you weren't even happy with the first one. Return it!)

Two Courses of Action

If you receive a gift that is wonderful, but you already have one, you have two courses of action.

The first is to thank the gift giver for the thoughtfulness and let the person know that the gift was "just what you always wanted!" Immediately get it out and show it. Say that you wanted one so much that you bought one for yourself! Or you asked for one for your birthday and you got it! Or the children surprised you with one for Valentine's Day! Or your mother-in-law made you one just like it (who would dare compete with that type of gift?)!

As difficult as it may seem to tell someone that you would like to return the gift or exchange it, the person will be thrilled to know that the gift was something that you really did love and would never dream of taking back if you didn't already have one! The person will also be very pleased to know that you thought enough about the hard-earned dollars not to turn it into a White Elephant that will lose money for the gift giver and for you, too.

Make a quiet exchange when you cannot tell the gift giver you already have one.

The second option is to make a Quiet Exchange. You do this when you can*not* bring yourself to tell the gift giver that you already have one, you just can't use the item, or you hate it. Use this method when you feel that you have no diplomatic excuse.

Look for a reliable store that handles the item and try

to exchange the gift. Usually, this is a wonderful solution because reliable stores see it as an opportunity to nurture customer relations, providing that they carry merchandise produced by the same company that manufactured your gift.

The problem arises when you can*not* find a store that carries the manufacturer of the gift item that you would like to exchange. You must go on a "safari" to find a store that does business with the manufacturer you need. If the store carries other items made by the same company, salespersons are usually more than happy to exchange your gift for something else.

Limited Choices

The big no-no to this choice is that it limits your shopping preferences because the store may not have what you want and you could be forced to take a store credit. You will get a store credit because the store can collect money from the manufacturer, but if the store does not have what you want, you are caught with your White Elephant in a state of limbo!

White Elephant Limbo—imagine an elephant flying around your favorite mall banging into trees, scraping his knees on the escalator, wandering about in a total state of helplessness. He is helpless because you have no recourse, no receipt, and nothing that you care to buy in exchange for the gift that you just don't want!

The merchant has nothing you want, and you know

that you do not want the White Elephant anymore! The merchant has no room for him in the stockroom!

Poor baby! Poor you! You can rescue him from limbo by spending your store credit when you find something you need, which could be NEVER.

You can exchange your gift for something you want (eventually). You will get a receipt for the item, your validation and proof, and finally—your gift! However, the exchange will still confine you to that same store in the event that the new item must be returned.

Only then will you have rescued your poor White Elephant and until then the White Elephant is a captive at the lost kiddie park and you are in financial limbo.

An exchange will confine you to the same store.

As closely attached as you and your elephant have become, you will soon find that not everyone loves him as much as you seem to think you do!

At the mall the night security guard complains that your White Elephant snores too much and keeps him awake when he tries to catch a few winks on his guard duty shift. The people at the food court complain that sales have been down because your White Elephant drinks out of their lemonade dispensers! They say when no one is looking, he uses his trunk for a straw and "slurps up" the profits!

Be Honest

It would have been easier to simply tell your friends or family that you already have one of whatever they gave you or that even though you love the thought, you would like to have the receipt to make a return! If you don't tell, your kids will.

CHAPTER 13

GIFT CERTIFICATES

In some circumstances you may have to take drastic measures to rescue your gift, especially when you get involved with the relative of your White Elephant—its cousin called gift certificate!

Gift Certificate—a piece of gift paper that has the capability of taking away all your shopper's rights. It is given with the best intentions and quite often drives the recipient to the brink of shopper's despair!

It can take the "Merry" out of Christmas, the "Happy" out of Hanukkah, the "anniversary" out of marriage, and divorce you and your favorite store!

I accept mine in "love" and usually spend them in frustration.

Generally, I return them to simplify things.

The Perfect Gift?

Most stores allow White Elephant Family Members to vacation at their establishments. In other words, most merchants issue gift certificates. They check the White Elephant Family Member into the computer (place of residence). They take money from the gift giver who opted for the "luxury gift" (which it should be) of presenting a special person with a shopping spree.

What a grand idea! If the store has what you want. If the store will let you spend your certificate as you wish. If the store will make it convenient for you to spend your gift certificate. If the store explains the gift certificate policies to the salespersons and the office force. If the store will give you money back to spend elsewhere if you do not find what you want.

After all, why was the gift certificate selected as a vehicle if all of these things were not part of the expectations of the gift giver for the giftee? I can*not* imagine!

If I shopped only at stores with excellent gift certificate policies, those that make gift certificates what they were designed to be—a pleasure, a luxury, a delight, a gift providing an experience that is fun, happy, relaxing, creative, thoughtful, and impressive—I would have no stores left in which to do my gift certificating!

Before the stores have registered the White Elephant's Relative into their guest quarters, which means that they have signed your giftee in as a recipient of their certificate shopping pleasures, you, the gift giver, have probably had to stand in line behind several people—each with nine items to be scanned—only to hear the salesperson say, "I'm sorry, but I can't do that here!"

"Why? Is it an illegal procedure?"

The person sounds relieved to have one less customer to serve and can barely control a little smirk that grows near the corners of the lips. You can be certain that the smirk is not a "Have a Good Day" smile because eventually the salesperson breaks into a huge grin that is well beyond the smile requirements for the store's "Have a Good Day" salutations!

You learn that you must go upstairs or downstairs to the Wrapping Paper Counter, which is never accessible but can be found by following people who look like they need the rest room services IMMEDIATELY!

Once again, you probably had to stand in line and eventually came face-to-face with someone who looked less than enthused about taking your money or filling out your gift certificates. On many occasions you even had to ask for an envelope for your gift. Once the woman handed me a plain white business envelope for my package wrapping and told me, "If you want gift wrap, pay for it!"

I should expect an appropriate envelope for my gift certificate. I hardly think that an appropriate designer envelope is beyond what should accompany the certificate as standard packaging. Beyond the initial presentation, a gift certificate is somewhat like getting nothing until you spend it. Consequently, packaging should be a priority for stores' gift certificates.

A Generous Gift

How did this lackluster opinion develop? One Christmas my husband gave me two $100 gift certificates for one of my favorite stores. He is a very generous man, and he thought that I would enjoy a shopping spree. As a seasoned husband and father, he thought it would be wiser to give me gift certificates than to try to decide on the sizes.

He figured the odds. If he picked too small, I would be upset. If he picked too big, I would be upset. If he didn't pick at all, I would be upset.

The perfect solution? Gift certificates! I was very happy with them, too, until I tried to spend them.

The first thought that came to my mind was that I had already purchased some lovely clothes and I could just pay my bill with the gift certificates! My husband had a great idea because he knew that I had lost the last of my "baby weight" after our fourth child and that I could use some new fashions. But I had already found some great sales, and I didn't really need more until the spring clothes blossomed on the scene. I loved the gift certificates because they freed my budget to buy the new bed that I wanted for our guest room. I was excited. Right after the holidays, I ran to the mall and went directly to the business office to use the certificates to pay the bill. Much to my surprise, the office told me that gift certificates can't be used to pay off an account.

"You can*not* be serious!" I said in total disbelief. "If I owed a bill at your store, and I refused to pay, you would suspend my credit card privileges, report my negligence to a collection agency to arrange for collection of delinquent funds, report my delinquency to a credit bureau, which would influence future credit decisions and, generally speaking, make my life uncomfortable!" But when I went to the store as a totally responsible customer who was anxious to pay a bill, I was informed a gift certificate could not be used as cash to pay a bill.

Gift certificates can't be used to pay off an account.

The store took my husband's cash, which it now had available to use to pay operational bills, to gain interest, and to force loyal customers to buy more merchandise. But when I said I could not believe that I could not use my gift certificate for such a responsible course of action—to pay my bill—the office person snapped, "READ THE SMALL PRINT!"

Sure enough. There it was in tiny little print designed to be read with a magnifying glass in language that spoke not to the average shopper but to a business law attorney (something like this): "Do not apply or allow the use of this toward any old debt or previous purchase . . . by said holder."

Oh, my goodness, I thought to myself. *I must be losing my touch. I've allowed myself to be distracted, and I forgot the obvious alternative. Return the gift certificate!*

I went home and asked my husband for the receipt. I

immediately went back to the business office, presented the receipt, and said, "I would like my money back!"

You guessed it! The office person said, "We can't do that."

By then I was getting up to ten on the receipt scale.

Receipt Scale—somewhat like the measure used to determine the severity of earthquakes. Ten is a serious rumbling that would require drastic action. In a gift certificate situation it would demand that the form of gift never be used again.

"We can*not* give you cash for a return."

"That is hard to believe, especially since we paid cash for the gift certificate."

"You will have to wait, and we will mail you a check within a month."

"No . . . I want my money NOW!"

I immediately asked to see the manager. I explained the situation. He said that I could not have my money because they were using a cash system that would not allow them to give refunds from the register. I asked how they gave change to their customers, and he said that was different because it would balance with the day's sales.

I said, "Under ordinary circumstances, a return is run through the register, and therefore, the return ticket validates the lack of cash."

"That is true!" agreed the manager. "If you had paid with a credit card, we would be able to refund your money immediately, but since you paid with honest-to-goodness real money, we can't do that!"

In sort of a whisper that was supposed to gain my trust, he pretended to let me in on a secret that no one else knew. He mumbled, "We have had a lot of theft problems lately. We just had to do something!"

On the surface that seems reasonable *except* that it penalizes the customer.

Let's remember I have not been able to begin to enjoy my gift yet. I have been asked to be the solution for the store's theft problems. Do you think my husband wanted all this to be a part of my Christmas gift? I have four children who have scattyeight activities that prevent me from having much mall time. The mall time that I am able to capture should be pleasant and lend itself to a wonderful shopping time meant to fulfill the agreement between the store and my husband (when it took his cash) for the privilege of allowing me to have a Merry Christmas gift certificate experience!

But wait. We shoppers are resilient! I had two $100 gift certificates.

I went back to the sales floor. I selected a pair of slacks that my son could use . . . key word *could*. I really would never have thought of spending the money for pants at that time, but if it meant that I might get my money back. . . . I handed the saleswoman the $100 gift certificate and waited for change.

Suddenly, I heard her say, "You can't use this to pay for these."

"Why not?" I asked.

"If you have a $100 gift certificate, you must spend more than $75 of the certificate to receive change."

I handed the pants back to her and told her to return them.

She said, "You can pay for them with a check, cash, or credit card!"

The situation had gotten totally out of hand—and it was my handful of money that it was being taken out of! Within minutes I was back at the office to speak to the manager, but by then the man in charge was at lunch.

I stood there explaining my situation to an entirely new personality and wasting more of my pleasurable shopping time.

The office person said, "If you really want to buy those pants (I never wanted the pants), we can reissue your gift certificate into $25 denominations."

"Great," I said with a smile. "DO IT!"

Within a half hour I was back downstairs with eight $25 gift certificates that I proceeded to spend on eight different pair of socks! I received about $23 back on each purchase, and then I returned each and every pair of socks—one pair at a time, one procedure at a time, one receipt at a time.

I immediately took all eight return slips to the customer service desk so that I could receive the money for the socks I returned (because as you remember they could not take cash for returns from the register).

Was it worth it? Most GIFT CERTIFICATELY!

Needless to say after an entire morning of aggravation, my shopping spree was over because it was time to pick up for my preschool car pool.

Maybe I'll try again Thursday morning while Chris is at school? No, that won't work. Jennifer has a dental appointment. Hmmmm . . . maybe next week? Nope . . . Scott has a field trip. Then when? I hope sometime before next Christmas!

A Complicated Gift

Surely, it can't be so difficult all the time! Maybe it was just that store?

Unfortunately, even my favorite stores have gift certificate policies that are not worthy in comparison to all of their other services. I believe that the storekeepers are the friends of the shoppers. I believe that most of the storekeepers do their best to make shopping a pleasant experience and respect the rights of the customer.

However, in the area of gift certificates when people have a problem, the complications involved are not worth the effort required.

Some people will have perfect experiences, but when they go "wrong," gift certificates are too much of a hassle considering the purpose for which they are designed.

You must be even more careful of certificates in small stores where there are too many variables like going out of business! Your mom was thoughtful enough to send you a gift certificate to your favorite little craft store. You plan a wonderful day. You rush and get the school lunches, throw everybody in the car, drop the children off at school, and meet your best friend for breakfast. Then you both hurry to the little shop. Surprise! It's gone. So are Mom's money and your Happy Birthday present!

Some of the smaller stores may be very quick to issue gift certificates, but they are very slow to honor them if a refund is necessary.

In a small store it is not at all unusual to have a problem finding exactly what you are looking for. It has the size but not the color. It has one, but you need two. You love the blue blazer, but the pants are the wrong shade.

Many times small stores are working from sale to sale just to pay the bills. When they say, "You can't have a refund," they mean they don't have your money anymore! That is also a problem with normal returns, but when it happens with a gift certificate, you have gotten absolutely nothing for your money.

A Grand Gift

The story I have just told you wasn't the first time that my husband had been disappointed with gift certificates. Actually, when he purchased the ones that we have just talked about, he thought that he had taken all the necessary precautions to make them a great gift.

The last time he bought me one, after our third baby, he bought a gift certificate at my favorite little dress shop, and he paid for it with a credit card. It was for $200, but it was all in one certificate. Once again, it was a grand idea until I tried to spend it.

I bought a wonderful suit. I absolutely loved it! You can see why Mr. Forst would think it was an idea worth trying again because the story I am about to tell you appeared to be an isolated incident.

The idea of a gift certificate as a cash sale at a big store with good return policies seemed like an idea that would be hard to beat even after the aggravation of the "third baby gift certificate story"! On the receipt scale it was probably about a five, which is not enough to make me a confirmed anticertificate person.

We went to dinner with friends, and I thoroughly enjoyed my new outfit. But the next time I wore the outfit,

I noticed that the zipper didn't run smoothly. I returned it to the store with my receipt, which amounted to more than the $200 that I had received in the gift certificate.

The first time I went back to the store the saleswoman said there was definitely something wrong with the zipper. She offered to call the other store to see if it had another skirt because her store had no more in that size. She discovered that the other store did not have the size I needed, either.

Since the store had nothing else that I wanted, I told her that I would like my money back. I was planning to try to find that same suit in one of the other stores in the mall. I had new shoes that matched the suit, I had a new purse, I had new hair clips, and I planned to find the same suit or one very much like it to recomplete the "third baby outfit."

That was when the trouble began. The saleswoman said that she could not refund my money because the outfit was purchased with a gift certificate. She knew that because on the receipt in the box that said method of payment, "Other" was checked. Next to it were written "Gift Certificate" and the salesperson's name.

I asked that famous return-it question, "Why not?"

She answered, "We just don't!"

"You just don't what?" I asked.

"We just don't give refunds on a gift certificate purchase."

That was a new one, even for me! "Who else can I see to discuss this?"

"No one," she said.

I asked to speak to her supervisor.

She said, "You'll have to come back. She isn't here."

"Can you call her, please?" I asked.

"No. It's her day off," she replied.
"Who else can I speak to?"
"No one," she retorted.
"She will be here tomorrow . . . Friday."

Beware of a store that authorizes money spent but negates money being returned without a special dispensation from an invisible person.

Friday I went back to the store to see the manager, and I was told that she would not be in until Tuesday and that the salesperson whose name was written on my receipt did not have the authority to refund my money.

Beware of a store that authorizes money spent but negates money being returned without a special dispensation from an invisible person. A store like that is using stall tactics to discourage you from pursuing the return issue. Those tactics only strengthen my resolve.

On Tuesday I arrived at the mall just as the doors opened—that is the very best time to return. I asked to speak to the supervisor.

"She isn't here yet," the saleswoman said.

"When will she be here?" I asked. "THIS IS RIDICULOUS. DO YOU KNOW HOW MANY TIMES I HAVE HAD TO COME DOWN HERE?"

"We're sorry. It is not our problem. We don't have the authority."

"Then you shouldn't be working here! If you can take my money, you should be able to give it back! If there is no one who can give a refund in six days, you should close your doors!"

The posted store return policy allowed returns to be made in a seven-day period for your money back. I knew that the "less than obvious" was going to become the "very obvious" in one more day.

I insisted that the salesperson (oh, person of little authority) write on my ticket that I had been trying to return the item and request a refund for my certificate for six days. The seventh day was approaching, and I wanted it documented that I had been trying to make a return for the past six days. I did not want them to attempt to enforce their seven-day-return-for-money policy. She thought it was strange, but she did sign the paper. And I had another salesperson initial it.

It was my receipt, and I could write on it (after all, didn't they write on it, too?). It was my only documentation. I figured I must protect my rights by documenting the document.

I went home and continued to call until I got someone to tell me that the invisible person would be in the store after 5:00 P.M. The salesperson also said that if I didn't have my husband's credit card, the store wouldn't be able to do the return. Obviously, the matter had been discussed with the invisible person who could not be reached.

I learned after that to stand my ground and to ask for the person who would be called in an emergency. That emergency person has to have the authority to authorize a return, just the way the person would be able to command an emergency situation by the telephone if the need arose. If they could reach her to get her schedule and discuss the situation, they could reach her for a customer.

At five o'clock I was at the desk of the store, and the supervisor had already written the credit. She only needed to run the card through the machine.

Despite all the hassle, I received no apology. She handed me the paperwork and said, "Thank you!"

I took the receipt, and put it into my wallet receipt file, and promised myself never to shop there again for any reason.

The small store has potential problems for efficient returns. In a small store very often the pitfalls of the gift certificate also apply to return procedures (especially cash sales). Try never to use cash anywhere the remotest possibility of a return might exist. If you have a dispute with a store, you can always settle it through the credit card company.

CHAPTER 14

TAKE IT TO THE TOP

KNOW YOUR "CHAIN OF COMMAND"!

While we were discussing the Kiddie Route, I mentioned if the children had a problem return, you were the beginning of their "chain of command."

Who is the beginning of your "chain of command"? You are the beginning, the middle, and the end of your "chain of command."

You will determine just how effective you will be in a return when you run into a difficult return, a difficult salesperson, a manager who thinks he owns the store, a service desk with no service, a business office with no supervisor, a department with no one in charge, or a business manager who doesn't know the business. All these possibilities exist in the return-it situation.

Appearance Matters

Your outward appearance can often act like body language and determine how you will be treated.

"Impossible!" you say.

I would like to believe that we have come full circle away from such judgments, but we have not! When I was a young person, I used to wonder why the older women and gentlemen would dress up to go to the stores. They would show up at the stores in coats with fur collars, hats, gloves, suits, and ties.

One day I began to notice that people who had been standing at the checkout counter in casual knock-around clothes were being overlooked while the salesperson asked a dressed-up person, "May I help you?"

I was astonished and outraged. I even spoke up and said, "She was next!"

Much to my amazement, the casually dressed "she" mumbled apologetically, "It's okay."

The salesperson never even offered to restore the casual dresser's place in the line.

I was fascinated. Could this be a factor in successful returning? I decided to try it and see.

When I dressed up to buy or return, I was treated more politely, served more successfully, smiled upon more frequently, and helped more willingly. Generally speaking, I had a great day at the mall.

When I shopped casual, I was treated proportionately poorly!

Once again my childhood history came to me in a vision, and I understood why all those people dressed up to shop. It was a most irritating discovery, a discovery, nevertheless, that could add to or subtract from your return-it dollars!

If you have a problem with this sort of discrimination, pretend that it is Halloween, dress up in your costume, and "Trick or Treat!" It's a "trick" that will put "treats" in your return-it bag and success into your shopping day! Then write a letter to the store manager and share your discoveries and experiences in this matter. It often makes a difference.

Follow Through

If this dress-up issue appears to be a factor, it seems fairly apparent that other factors like self-confidence, determination, simple language, positive statements, and following through the entire "chain of command" would directly affect your success in returning.

If you have a problem, ask for a salesperson. If the salesperson has a problem, request a supervisor. Don't be afraid to proceed through the floor manager to the store manager up to the business office straight through to the president of the company. Fear not. The owner will really try to help.

The closer you get to the top of the "chain of command," the more often you will experience "satisfaction guaranteed"!

Practice your presentation before you go to the store. Briefly write down what you want. Prepare the answer to the question, "May I help you?" Be ready to state what you need and what you want the store to do.

Be specific, factual, firm, unruffled (always calm), focused on the issue, and undaunted. Persevere and pursue. Ask for and write down names with the confidence born from your right and the receipt! Then RETURN IT!

> *The closer you get to the top of the "chain of command," the more often you will experience "satisfaction guaranteed."*

"That's Different!"

I once spent an hour of returning energy taking back a blouse and bow tie to a specialty shop in the mall. Earlier in the day I found a blouse to match a skirt that sat in my closet for months because there was no blouse in all the house to match the skirt, no special shirt to go with the skirt that sat in the closet for months.

I thought the shirt was perfect, but just in case I asked, "If this shirt that I bought to go with the skirt that sat in the closet for lack of a shirt doesn't go with the skirt for which I bought the shirt, can I bring it back?"

The saleswoman assured me that I could bring back the shirt that I bought to go with the skirt that sat in the closet for lack of a shirt . . . and the bow tie, too, if they didn't do.

They didn't and I did take them back that very afternoon! I walked in with my receipt with the bag, which had not even been unpacked because it was apparent by holding the shirt to the skirt that the color was off.

The saleswoman was the same one, and I said, "This color shirt was wrong!" I fully expected her to say, "Here's your money back!"

Instead she said, "You can*not* return that!"

I reminded her that she had said that I could and that I had paid cash for the purchase to make it easy to void the sale if the need arose. Then she said that even if she could allow me to return the shirt and tie, she could not give me back my cash.

I took care of the basic issue first. "Your sign says that all items are returnable within seven days with the receipt, unworn, for complete 'satisfaction' guaranteed!'

"You are right," she said.

"Then you will refund my money," I stated.

"Well, I guess," she said.

"Well, I guess. What kind of a return policy is that?"

It is called a PRP—poor return policy. It is hazardous to your budget! If a store has PRP, stay away! It is incurable and contagious. You will always suffer the consequences in your purse strings.

She handed me a form to fill out about the return.

I signed it.

She signed it, and I waited for my money.

About that time she started to wait on another customer.

I was nicely dressed, too. I excused myself and said "My money?"

The saleswoman said abruptly, "I told you that I can*not* give you your money. You will receive a check in the mail in about two weeks!"

"Two weeks! I gave you the money—$48.95—not more than two hours ago!" I said.

"I'm sorry, but I can*not* open the register."

"You opened it to take my money," I stated.

"That's different!"

Different is not acceptable! Stores do not bend return policies for your idiosyncrasies, and different has no place in their policies! Either it is, or it isn't!

"Who else may I speak to about this?"

I began to get the whole list: "No one. We have no one to call in an emergency. Our manager is out of town. I'm in charge."

I responded, "Who would you call in case of robbery or a fire?"

Soon I was getting stammering and "Well, ahhhhs!"

I had my answer. There was a warm body a phone call away who could resolve this dispute! Stand your ground.

"Please call your emergency number for me," I asked.

"I can't call that number, and I can't give you your money."

"I'll just stand here in the store until you get a minute to call, and when you do reach the invisible emergency person, I want to speak to her!"

"She is out of town!"

"If there were a fire, I am certain that she would respond from wherever she is, wouldn't she?"

"That's different," she said.

There we were again. "What is different is that I'm going to stand here for as long as it takes for you to try to call your manager!"

A half hour later she called. She got an answering

machine and left a message! Three minutes later I was taking to the manager. She said that she could not open the register. She said that they had had theft problems and that cash could not be removed from the register as a store method to curb thievery.

"How do you make change for customers?" I asked.

She said, "That's different."

What was truly different was that the store needed my money to make ends meet. Less than six months later, it was out of business!

Finally, the manager told the saleswoman to go ahead and refund my cash. Had the incident occurred just before the store went out of business, I might never have gotten my refund check in the mail! A clear case of incurable PRP!

"Chain of command" means just that—a long line of options over which YOU are in charge, in command, in control. In every way, it is up to you to say, "Take it back!"

Using all your return-it skills, methods, and hints, you must protect your rights!

Your Children's "Chain of Command"

Kiddies "can, too," return things. But in the "chain of command" sometimes their first link is you! I have taught my children their return-it skills according to ages and readiness, but unfortunately, no matter how prepared young people are to practice their skills, there are always some adults who are not so adult about the way they treat children in the shopping environment.

The sale is never over until the customer is "satisfied" was never meant to be qualified by age or the lack of it. There is nothing in the "satisfaction guaranteed" promise that ever said, "Unless you are under eighteen!"

Unfortunately, some adults are threatened by young people with great shopping skills. They feel that the young people pose a threat to their authority, position, and effectiveness. Somehow the adults feel that the children are challenging their abilities.

Adult salespeople take a young person's return as a personal affront. That's where you come into their "chain of command." You are their little backup insurance policy.

My older daughter, Kristen, received an expensive purse as her main Christmas gift. It was all she really wanted. To her, it was perfect until the shoulder strap broke.

Kristen went to the store with her purse in the store bag, with her receipt, with her confident return-it skills, only to be told by the saleswoman she couldn't exchange or refund. The store no longer carried products by that manufacturer! And "Have a Nice Day!"

Kristen told the woman that she understood the store had a problem with the manufacturer, but that it should not cause her any difficulty. She bought the purse in good faith from the store, and she expected it to honor the return agreements with customers.

The saleswoman threatened to call the manager.

Kristen said, "Please do."

The manager told her all the same things, but she offered to give Kristen the name and address of the company that manufactured the purse "in case" Kristen wanted to "see what they could do. That is what you should do!"

Kristen stated firmly, "You do not carry the purse. I do not want a different one. I want a refund. Please credit it back to this card!"

The manager refused.

Kristen promised to be back!

Within the hour we were back at the store. I immediately asked for the manager. I told her who I was and what I wanted.

She gave me the same explanation that she gave Kristen, but this time we were eye-to-eye, adult-to-adult, with several other customers listening at the purse counter.

Oddly enough, one woman there was getting ready to select a bag when she overheard the conversation and said, "Are you trying to return your bag, too? I had a problem, and they were making me select a different purse altogether. I don't really want this one, but . . ."

The woman spoke up and said to the manager, "I want my money, too!"

"We're really not authorized to do that," the manager said.

"You were authorized to sell this purse," I said.

"Until you have satisfied each customer, you are the one who must work it out with the manufacturer!"

"If we refund your money . . . we may not be reimbursed," she argued.

"That may be true, but that is your responsibility and loss. It certainly should not be Kristen's problem or the other purse buyer's problem!"

They both received refunds.

Kristen's efforts were an example for two adults! Kristen said all the things that I eventually had to repeat. They forced us to make two trips to do what she had done correctly in the first place.

The saleswoman and the manager had no authority to make a decision that deprived a young person or any other customer of the joy of the gift. They inconvenienced and embarrassed their loyal customers. The manager even suggested to Kristen, "If you write to the manufacturer, you would probably do better if you didn't mention the store where you purchased it. The people in the returns department won't care where you got it. They'll recognize their own product."

Kristen knew that she had been treated badly, and she came to her insurance link in her "chain of command!" Together we corrected the incident.

They apologized for the misunderstanding. I assured them that it had not been a misunderstanding. We understood perfectly that their misplaced salesmanship had disturbed my daughter and upset my purse strings.

You must understand clearly and defend diligently your rights by using your return-it skills.

Knowing you are being treated badly is the first step! Now go through your "chain of command." It begins and ends with you!

Communicate with the Proper Person

Because I considered this incident a case of shopping abuse, I made a formal complaint in the form of a letter to the store manager. When establishments say, "Tell us how we are doing," they usually mean it, and it is a very important tool for Store-to-Door Communications!

Store-to-Door Communications—an invisible little phone line that enables your shopper's thoughts to flow through the line to the store people in charge who could make a difference.

I have heard people apologize to salespersons when they lost their tempers over a shopping issue. They say, "I'm not really mad at you, but you're the one who's here!"

It might make you feel better to get your complaints off your chest, but complaining to, hollering at, or getting angry with the wrong people does nothing to promote Store-to-Door Communications. If your customer service lines are scrambled, go to the appropriate person to complain. Otherwise, your anger is counterproductive, and your manners will be questionable. If you go away angry, you may go away for good. Without "satisfaction guaranteed" poor communications will keep things from going out of the store through the door!

Use your energy and effort toward productive Open Store-to-Door Communications! No one wants that kind of Store-to-Door Communications more than the reputable stores. It is important to you, but it is vital to their existence. There are more reputable business establishments than not.

Tender Love and Credit

Whenever I run into "the best of the rest," I love to give them TLC—Tender Love and Credit (where credit is due)! You might say, "Credit others as they credit you!"

Tell your return-it stories. Share them with other shoppers. Word of mouth is still the best form of advertisement.

> ***Whenever I run into "the best of the rest," I love to give them TLC—Tender Love and Credit.***

If you doubt it, think of the last story that you heard. Did anyone doubt it? "No, everyone talked about it!" Return-it tales are motivational, emotional, devotional, and historical accounts of our lives!

Our receipts are actually history books in the making! I have receipts from the furniture we bought twenty years ago, clothes we bought five years ago, three-year-old toys, seven-year-old appliances, and two-year-old televisions.

Why? They tell stories—warranty stories, insurance stories, quality stories, and love stories of lives shared. I love to take a trip down memory lane over the years through our receipts.

My favorite TLC story happened because my uncle came to visit. He sat down in our "good" lounge chair, pulled up the foot rest, and went head over heels.

For the last five years of its fifteen-year life, we were always telling the children "not to jump on the good chair." They would always say, "Okay, Mom!" and proceed to jump on the green chair!

"Did you hear me?" I would say. I wondered subconsciously why I always had to repeat myself. Deep down inside I knew that the chair was older than it ought to be. I always chose to let their jumping be one of those little things you mention (as your parently duty) but prefer to ignore!

Now I know that they would never have jumped on the "good" chair if they had known where it was, but they knew beyond a shadow of a doubt that it certainly couldn't have been the green chair, so they were safe.

The green chair happened to be the only chair left in the room because through our corporate moves, we had started to weed out the old furniture. How much older could the stuff have gotten before it got into the "slightly used" or "you're allowed to jump on it" category? Obviously not too much because it just rolled over and died in the line of duty.

This little episode reminded us that the "good" furniture had long since passed the mandatory retirement age. Thus the hunt began.

I wanted something light and bright. Realistically, a family of six should be looking for something in the mud and ketchup shades. I knew in my heart, though, that my children were different. I could have a white sectional sofa in my family room. After all, didn't we have the last sofa for fifteen years before we even noticed that it was getting a little tired? My children could manage to keep a lovely light fabric spotless. Wrong!

After we looked and looked and looked and looked, we decided to buy nothing. Since there was no perfect fabric for my stage in life, we bought some huge throw pillows for the floor in front of the television and placed a huge wooden trestle table with trestle benches in front of the fireplace for all projects, coloring, homework, and cereal eating.

Everything was washable, polishable, and comfortable. Amen! It was divine inspiration!

Until the next corporate move to the Land of Great Rooms . . . Florida! Suddenly, we were reduced to human choices again. We had to pick out furniture because the center of the house was the family room.

We visited every store in Orlando. We decided that we could solve the ketchup and mud decor problem by buying leather. But it was very expensive!

"In the long run it's cheap," chirped the saleswoman.

"I sent my old leather sofa to college with my son," chimed in . . . another salesperson.

Leather was perfect, but maybe we should buy something less expensive and throw it away after a few years. That theory won out after we had looked and looked and looked again until we decided to forgo everything we had decided to look for because one enchanted evening we were wandering through the furniture section of a popular department store (not looking for furniture) on our way to the escalator.

As we were going up I looked down and noticed a big banner that said, "At least 50 percent off all floor merchandise!" We were tired. We were hungry. We were having company for the weekend.

A huge seafom-and-mauve love seat and sofa jumped out at us! They had touches of bamboo. We had temporary insanity because we were contemporary country people, Wedgewood blue-and-beige people, preppy little print people, traditional stripe people, who went home that night straight "off the floor" with a love seat and sofa that we would both learn to hate before the morning sunrise.

We had promised ourselves light, bright, and neutral, and we were absolutely certain after a two-year search that the tropical version of the old Colonial basket-and-bird print (which we lived with for years) was the answer to our "new look." Within fifteen minutes we had paid for and carried out a tropical print that was unique to us and common to half the hotel lobbies of the Southeast!

On the ride home we began to have moments of sanity, and we could be heard saying to each other, "This will be great!"

"Oh, yes, we will love this look."

"I can't wait to see them in the house," said Jack.

I said, "Yes, you could! We could have waited an eternity for that look!" I felt ill!

"You are being ridiculous!" I admonished myself. "There's nothing wrong with this set! You are having prenuptial jitters!"

It's practically the same thing. Some marriages don't last as long as some sofas stay in people's homes! Couples divorce, but people learn to live with their sofas!

Our friends restrained their gasps and tried to turn them into positive good houseguest compliments.

As soon as they left I called my friend Sara who happens to be a world-class designer, and screamed, "HELP! NOW!"

Sara said that sort of impulse buying is not unusual for shoppers. She has seen signs of it in her clients, but since she knows what to expect, she is usually able to soothe their impulse-buying outbursts and get them back to the drawing board *before* they buy something they will grow to hate!

We tried new accessories. "Nope!" We tried new

kitchen furniture to see if we could match something "out of character" with something even more "out of character."

Sara said, "Stop! This isn't working!"

I couldn't! I was getting obsessed with this chase to find the perfect solution to a problem sofa with which it seemed I'd be spending fifteen years (in jail). I dreamed that it would disappear!

After about two weeks I found myself peeking around the corner as I would get up in the morning, squinting and hoping that someone had stolen it. No one ever did!

One Saturday Mr. Forst looked out over his newspaper and said, "You know, Patty, we might have a problem with this furniture!"

Oh, my goodness. He hated it, too. My prayers had been answered!

"It's really beautiful," he sputtered. "But it's been hard to find 'stuff' to make this 'Thing' match."

In less than a month we had begun to call the furniture the "Thing." And even though the sale was an "at least 50 percent offer," it was upsetting to think that the only accessories that you could find to coordinate with the Thing fit in the category labeled "stuff."

"Maybe some new end tables would help," said Mr. Forst. We hopped into the car and ran down to one of the furniture stores that carried end tables that were "kinda" the kind that went with furniture "kinda" like what we had bought.

The salespersons all knew us, and so the one who was up had to do the honors. We proceeded through a long series of "These are nice!"; "Whattaya think of wicker?"; "That color looks good."; "Maybe these will go."

We found a set that looked like "the ones."

"I don't know," I said. I really did know. I thought I hated them, but then there was a time (for one fleeting moment) that I thought I loved the sofas.

"Great. Let's try them!"

"When would you like us to deliver them?" the salesperson asked.

"Deliver? Oh, no! We'll just take them along with us," said Mr. Forst.

As I paid, he put them in the car, and within the hour we had looked for, purchased, and returned our end tables.

As we sat in the family room, we played peekaboo over the Sunday paper trying to see if we could see the other person looking at the Thing and wondering what we were going to do with it.

Suddenly, it came to me in a vision! We needed living room furniture, too. Maybe, the family room furniture would look better in the living room! "I'll try it!"

As soon as Father Forst left for his golf match, I went to work. I dragged the living room furniture into the family room. "Ohhhh!" It felt like home again! Then I pulled the family room furniture to the living room. It was looking better already.

I carefully arranged everything. The living room looked very pink. The furniture looked very cramped. All in all it looked great because for the first time in a month I didn't have to look at it in the family room anymore. Actually, since we hardly ever used the living room, with any luck I would never have to see it again.

When Mr. Forst arrived home, he walked in, sat down, and sighed in relief as he gently patted our old familiar soon-to-be-retired, but-for-the-moment-reinstated sofa.

"What made you think of this? It's a great idea! We never realized that this stuff might not suit the family room (the understatement of the year!). But we don't use the living room that much!"

Suddenly, I had had enough! I was astonished that we had put ourselves through all that anxiety and aggravation, not to mention that we had spent a month describing our furniture with such words as *the Thing, stuff,* and *not too bad*.

The only spark of happy descriptive language was expressed when we got the stuff out of our sight.

I was coming to my senses!

It was Sunday. The department store was open. I had gone to church. Maybe God read my mind and inspired me to get my gumption back!

God helps those who help themselves even if they think they don't deserve it! Don't deserve it? That was it! It was our fault! We selected incorrectly. We bought impulsively. We didn't follow our guidelines. So we deserve to live with it for the next fifteen years!

There, I said it!

Right?

WRONG!

I had forgotten the other banner that hung over the door that said "SATISFACTION GUARANTEED!" It didn't say "SATISFACTION GUARANTEED" only if you buy two! Or when you know that it will fit! Or if you are certain that it's right! Or as long as you buy the one you like! Or every Wednesday but not Friday! Or at certain times that suit us! Or unless of course we say so!

It said "SATISFACTION GUARANTEED" all the time, every day of the week, for any honest reason with your receipt!

I had my receipt! We had a problem, but the store policy makers knew that that was part of the shopping process. They didn't want occasional sales. They wanted Happy Camper Customers!

Still I was nervous as I called and asked to speak to our salesman (who had been very helpful and was about to lose a commission). I said, "This furniture isn't working. . . . We would like to return it."

He said, "Let me get that paperwork." He returned to the phone and said, "We'll pick it up on Wednesday. We are so sorry that it didn't work. When you get your fabric warranty, please bring it in! We will cancel it. You will get a refund in the mail! Please have your receipt ready for the truck driver. He will be there sometime in the afternoon."

On Wednesday when the truck driver arrived, the driver and his helper came in, went directly to the furniture, and uncovered the stuff. We had covered it with sheets just the way they did in the old movies for storage because we didn't want to see it anymore. We wanted it out of our lives, but the only way that would happen was to block it out of the budget through the return-it process! That process was going on in our living room as the gentlemen removed the furniture from our home.

I walked to the truck with my receipts and what to my wondering eyes did appear? An entire truckload of furniture!

"Do you have to deliver all that now?"

"Oh, no," he laughed, "we picked all this up today!"

"SATISFACTION GUARANTEED" is assured by the ultimate shopping tool . . . the store.

A store that stands behind its customers, a store that nurtures its customers, a store that allows its customers, a store that pleases its customers, a store that develops its customers, a store that likes its customers, a store that looks beyond one sale, a store that looks to the future with happy people shopping!

When they said, "Thank you for shopping with us," they meant it!

When we said, "You are welcome," we meant it! You are welcome back into our home as we shop in the future!

SATISFACTION FOR ALL GUARANTEED!

Care enough to share, to compliment, to complain, to discuss.

The best advertisement is word of mouth. Tell your return-it tales.

Share your "once upon a receipt" stories.

Broadcast TLC situations.

Comment on PRP disease.

You are the measure of things to come. Care enough to share, to compliment, to complain, to discuss.

The ultimate tool (the store) is only as good as its STORE-TO-DOOR COMMUNICATIONS with YOU!

CHAPTER 15

HAPPY CAMPER CUSTOMERS

IT'S A MONEY SAVER.

When you feel that you have the power to correct any buying mistakes that you make, then you develop an entirely new approach to returning.

It's mathematical. If subtraction is the inverse of addition, then returning is the inverse of buying.

BUYING + RETURNING = SHOPPING

SHOPPING + MONEY = BUYING

SHOPPING + RETURNING = MONEY

WHICH . . . ALGEBRAICALLY SPEAKING EQUALS "SATISFACTION GUARANTEED!"

Profit for Everyone

Returning equals profit for everyone. Even the merchants benefit from my Return-It Theory because by responsive and responsible return policies, they develop a business relationship with happy customers. When people know that they can return just about anything to the stores, the merchants have converted occasional sales to unknown people into regular business from satisfied customers. The stores may lose a sale, but they gain profit in the long run when they foster Happy Camper Customers!

Happy Camper Customer—one who goes to the store with his camping equipment to wait for a great sale but who also will drive fifty miles to that same store to shop even when there is no sale!

A Loyal, Happy Camper Customer

When I am shopping, I often buy something that I think will be suitable (even if I'm not sure) because I shop only at stores where I know that I can return it.

By responsive and responsible return policies, merchants develop a business relationship with happy customers.

Stores that know shopping is a process. Stores that know shopping doesn't imply that customers actually know what they are looking for or want. Stores where the customers are not afraid to shop again. That is the key—again and again and again!

Even though there are always jokes about some of us being professional shoppers, the fact remains that most of us do not have hours to shop. Time is a true luxury in today's fast-paced society. When we do get time, we want to get the shopping done!

Consequently, if I'm not sure about a purchase, I get it! If I am right in my choice, my shopping is done! If I am wrong, I return it!

If you don't buy it, you have to go back to the store at another time anyway to get whatever you went to buy in the first place.

The storekeeper has a fifty-fifty chance of breaking even, a better than average chance to make a sale, and a marvelous opportunity for great public relations.

You *Can* Return Big Things

Many people subconsciously dismiss their right to return by coming up with all sorts of reasons why they can*not* return something! After hearing about our "satisfaction guaranteed" story or our TLC (Tender Love and Credit) story, a good friend of ours said, "I didn't know that! You are kidding! They really did that! I'm glad I learned that! Gosh . . . if you can do that, so can I. You mean you can return big things?"

Charlie laughed, "Oh, but I've had it too long, haven't I?"

That's one of the excuses that people give for not returning it sooner! People who honestly have a complaint about big items think that because they are big and expensive, they can*not* return them!

Barb and Charlie had been sleeping on a less-than-comfortable mattress that was somewhat like our "good" green chair. Finally, they, too, honored the Mandatory Retirement Age Agreement for all mattresses, and they treated their backs to a new one.

The purchase was an occasion because it was Charlie's answer to springing out of bed again in the morning. Except for one thing—the new wonder mattress did not seem to help. In fact, it seemed that Barb's back began to hurt her, too. As a joke we all had assured him that he was expecting too much because his back problems were caused not by the mattress but simply by old age.

It is never too big to go back, and it is never too late to check your guarantees and warranties!

Barb's backache was a sympathy pain for her hubby's plight! Since we were all included in the old age joke, we thought that Charlie would take it with a grain of salt. On the contrary, we had convinced him back pain was a thing of his past, present, and future.

After hearing the return-it furniture story, Charlie sprang from his chair and said, "You mean you can do that?" Wait a minute! In his surprise, he had forgotten everything we had taught him! He had jumped from his chair!

"My spring hasn't sprung yet. . . . It can't be my age; it must be the new mattress!" He said in amazement.

We had all been friends too long for any of us to be guilty of receiptlessness. Barbara had the proof of purchase. That proof of purchase provided Charlie with Limited Warranty Information, which enabled him to return the mattress on a twenty-year warranty after two years prorated to the cost of "almost free."

It is never too big to go back, and it is never too late to check your guarantees and warranties!

CHAPTER 16

NOTHING TO LOSE

My brother-in-law, Al, inspired me to write this last chapter because when he came to visit, he dragged out a pair of tennis shoes that he had worn for about one hour until he realized they hurt his feet. He purchased them for a trip because he wanted to walk in the evenings for his exercise. Since they hurt his feet, he brought them along to give to Scott. Remember Scott, our older son, who was about to inherit Grandpa's Sunday shirt? Well, now the young man was soon to inherit a pair of very adult and practical-looking tennis shoes.

When Scott saw the shoes, he said, "Uncle Alfred, you should really return them!"

With a sheepish grin, Uncle Al said, "Yeah . . . yeah I know!" And in a whisper not meant for my ears he said, "I don't have my receipt! I don't know where I got them."

We all bellowed!

"What!" I said. "My own brother-in-law didn't do any of the things we are always talking about!"

"Well, I thought they would be okay," he said. "I didn't think I would need my receipt."

"Those shoes cost a lot of money, and now you still don't have any to wear! We will try to return them here!"

Scott could be heard saying a quick "Thank You, God!"

Well, even I couldn't help Alfred because the shoes were a brand that our stores didn't carry, and that made an exchange out of the question. We had no receipt. We had no manufacturer that was recognizable in our area, and it appeared that we had no options. Did we?

As we were driving home, I said, "Al, after your vacation, you are going to march yourself back to the stores where you think you might have bought these shoes. If you can't find the right one, you are going to try to find a store that carries them and ask if the storekeeper would be so kind as to exchange them. It has been less than thirty days since you bought them, and they obviously have a defect in the lining. You are in the hands of the storekeeper. Give it a try. You have nothing to lose! It is perfect opportunity to practice your skills and to see what happens!"

We all have experienced the Lack of a Receiptitis, the Thirty-Day Doldrums, Original Packitis. But then again we all have had a cold, a fever, the flu, an occasional "achhoo" that threatened our health temporarily, just as a case of receiptlessness can endanger our return abilities for the moment! We have survived!

You Have Nothing to Lose

The worst that can happen has already happened. If they won't take it back now, you haven't lost another thing! Try. Gather your return and any materials that might help. Plan a route in case you've gathered some new items in your return-it cube. If it is a store return where you have a credit card, that might help!

Have your card ready. Take the item back. Explain your problem. Ask for a credit to your card. Remember your "chain of command"! An incomplete return will usually require a supervisor's approval.

Expect to use the skills that are still available to you! Know what to expect and work with the system. The higher you go, the more they know about exceptions to the rules!

When you get a judgment on your return item, if the store refuses to take the item back by giving credit to your credit card account, in essence a "cash" return, take a store credit. Under the circumstances, the store is being very generous. The store has no way of knowing whether the item is its own or not! For maintaining good public relations and building Happy Camper Customers, the store is usually happy to give an equal exchange or a store credit. Even though accepting a store credit may be a little inconvenient, you have at least saved your money for a future purchase that you really want.

> *Know what to expect and work with the system.*

You'll be happy to know that Uncle Alfred called the day after he got home and said that he remembered where he bought the shoes. He took the shoes to the manager, and he agreed that they were defective. He gave Alfred another pair. Even without the receipt, the manager recognized his merchandise, and he was more than happy to turn Al into a Happy Camper Customer who will no doubt buy all his shoes at that establishment and recommend it to all his friends.

Beware No Returns for Cash or Credit

I, too, had an experience where I had nothing to lose by returning. I bought outfits that I thought were perfect for my daughters and put them in their Easter baskets. They had seen them at the mall at one of the stands rented to individual specialty shops. The mall rents floor space to shops that aren't big enough for store space but need mall exposure with a cute display concept. Generally speaking, overhead and expenses predispose these shops to endorse one type of return policy—no returns for cash or credit.

Despite their PRP (poor return policy), I thought the

outfits were still Easter basket prizes because the girls had already tried them on for style, size, and color.

Unfortunately, I didn't know that the style was so popular that two different stands carried the sets. I shopped at the wrong stand!

Therein lies the problem. Whatever shopping situation you think won't occur WILL! I had two baskets filled with outfits that needed to go back to a portable shop that had no real return policy.

I went back to the mall. Just as I expected, the salesperson said no to a refund and insisted on an even exchange.

I thought, *Oh, well, I'll shop for next year!* But there was nothing I wanted, and I was nervous about gift buying at a shop that had PRP disease!

The only reason I shopped there in the first place was that I thought the gifts were pretested.

I had established my No Buying at Stand Stores Policy ages ago. I had purchased barrettes at one of the stand stores only to discover that the salesperson would not refund my money, even on defective merchandise. The barrette clips were sharp and cut my daughter's hair. The shop offered new barrettes, but they weren't any better. They had sharp edges that would cut, too!

Another time a friend purchased a wristwatch that was guaranteed against defects for one year. The watch broke in a month, and by then the store was no longer in business. With those situations in mind you can appreciate that I thought things were pretty bleak. I tried to repurchase things that I thought might do, could fit, or were kinda pretty.

Try as I would, the "almost okay" items wouldn't

add up to the purchase price of the original items. The salesperson offered a store credit to make up the difference. That was it! It took awhile, but I finally said, "Wait a minute! Stop! This is crazy! Is there someone else that I could speak to about this?"

A tall man came over from the next stand. He had been watching the whole process. He was the owner of several shops. I told my story while lamenting the fact (politely) that I was being forced to do business with the store even though I really needed to make a return in order to repurchase the items I really wanted. "Don't you think you would do more business if word got out that you were one of the few stores of this type that had Happy Camper Customer Policies?"

He smiled and said, "I guess you are right. Give her money back!"

I asked, "What have I got to lose?" and I found out that the answer was, "Nothing!" In the worst return-it situation a simple case of perseverance was rewarded with success.

Persevere!

Don't give up! Return it!
You absolutely will lose if you do not return it.

> ***Perseverance can lead to success.***

You have a fifty-fifty chance if you try.

Receipts are great, there is no doubt.
But should you lose 'em
try without to make the return.
No receipt for the wilted roses?
Take 'em back in exchange for posies.

All the routines are here for you.
You just have to carry through.
I hope that you will learn
From what you've read, how to return

JUST ABOUT ANYTHING!